T.V. Reddy's Poetry
The Pulse of Life
Essential Readings

By T. Vasudeva Reddy, PhD

Foreword by K.V. Dominic

Modern History Press
Ann Arbor

T.V. Reddy's Poetry - The Pulse of Life: Essential Readings.
Copyright © 2017 by T. Vasudeva Reddy, PhD. All Rights Reserved.

2nd Printing – January 2018

From the *Essential Readings* series at Modern History Press.

ISBN 978-1-61599-344-4 paperback
ISBN 978-1-61599-370-3 hardcover
ISBN 978-1-61599-346-8 eBook

Library of Congress Cataloging-in-Publication Data

Names: Vasudeva Reddy, T., 1943- author.
Title: T. V. Reddy's poetry : the pulse of life / by T. Vasudeva Reddy, PhD.
Description: Ann Arbor, MI : Modern History Press, 2017. | Series: Essential
  readings | Includes index.
Identifiers: LCCN 2017022995 (print) | LCCN 2017032608 (ebook) | ISBN
  9781615993468 (ePub, PDF, Kindle) | ISBN 9781615993444 (pbk. : alk.
paper) | ISBN 9781615993703 (hardcover : alk. paper)
Classification: LCC PR9499.3.V3743 (ebook) | LCC PR9499.3.V3743 A6 2017
  (print) | DDC 821/.914--dc23
LC record available at https://lccn.loc.gov/2017022995

Published by:
Modern History Press
5145 Pontiac Trail
Ann Arbor, MI 48105

info@ModernHistoryPress.com
www.ModernHistoryPress.com

Distributed by Ingram International (USA/CAN/AU), Bertram's Books
(UK/EU)

Contents

Pensive Memories **51**

Gliding Ripples **67**

Foreword

When I was contacted through email by the publisher Victor R. Volkman to write a foreword to this book, I didn't have to think a minute to give the reply. Rather, I took it as a great honour as well as my duty to write something on the great poetry of my bosom elder friend, Prof. T. V. Reddy. He is not just my friend, but an elder brother and mentor. This foreword is being written when my edited book of his poetry is being printed by Authorspress, New Delhi. That book is *The Poetic Art of T. V. Reddy: New Perspectives,* which contains twenty-four research articles by renowned professors, writers and research scholars.

My association with Prof. T.V. Reddy started in 2010. He was introduced to me by my friend, who is highly regarded Indian English poet, Dr. D. C. Chambial. We had several phone calls and I was much impressed by Prof. Reddy's depth in English literature and poetry. His gentle, loving words were pleasant to the ears. As Secretary of the GIEWEC (Guild of Indian English Writers, Editors and Critics), which was established in October 2010, I invited him for the two day national level literary festival to be conducted at St. Teresa's College, Kochi (Kerala) on 17th and 18th, 2011. Thus I met him for the first time on 16th September, 2011. Despite being a senior, established writer he talked to me and others with great humility, simplicity and gentleness. We were all very eager to listen to his invaluable talks, and reading of beautiful poems. My association with him continued more fervently, and he was unanimously elected as the President of the GIEWEC in the next general body meeting and literary festival conducted in Mumbai, in 2012. From then, he has been serving the Guild as the Honorary President.

Prof. T. V. Reddy shines like a unique star among the great contemporary Indian poets in English, and deserves a place very close to Prof. Jayanta Mahapatra, among the best English poets in the country now. It is really tragic and ironical that Prof. Reddy is less read and studied by his own compatriots than by poetry lovers abroad. The awards and honorary D.Litt. he was conferred from WAAC (San Francisco) indicate this fact. It is really surprising that Prof. Reddy's poetry has not been included in the syllabus of schools, colleges and universities in India. His literary output is not small—twelve collections of poems, two novels, three critical books and a grammar book. And he has been publishing books from 1982. Being an English teacher, I had to teach poems of many Indian English poets at undergraduate and postgraduate level. Prof. Reddy's poetry seems to me far superior to many poems which were taught. He, like many other contemporary Indian English poets, is a victim of dirty politics. It is not the worth that is counted very often. Same is the case with awards also. He should have been considered for the Sahitya Akademy award from the government of India.

What makes Prof. Reddy distinct from other contemporary poets is that he is a meeting point of the past and the new—conventional, structured, rhymed poetry and the present, unrhymed free verse. He started writing English poems in reaction to the outputs of some of the so-called leading English poets in the country. Rhythm in his poems is as musical as ripples of a brook. Other contemporary English poets seldom use rhymes so natural and sensible to the lines. He in fact reminds me of the leading Romantic and Victorian poets with regard to his lyrical qualities—the craft of rhymes, assonance and alliteration, and the use of imagery. Prof. Reddy is a rural poet, portraying the beauties of his village—landscape, flora and fauna, innocent people, animals and birds etc. Since he shifts his life from village to town very often, we also find urban scenes and their beauties in some of his poems. Being a social critic, many of his poems are satirical, while some lampoon the hypocrisy and parasite mentality of politicians. Prof. Reddy, spiritual and pious to the core, has written some excellent poems dealing with metaphysical and philosophical themes. Using very simple vocabulary, he conquers the minds of readers, and allures them to voyage through his poems, one after the other till the end of the book. Reputed Indian English poet and critic, P. C. K. Prem, notes in his research paper "Prototypical Quest and Ultimate Futility: Poetry of T. V. Reddy" that "He does not withdraw memories and moral instances, but at the same time a didactic essence permeates many lyrics, but most of the time one detects incantation, a little ornamentation and undertones of emotions when he resurrects rural atmosphere" (*The Poetic Art of T. V. Reddy: New Perspectives* 59).

Now coming to this book, it contains a rich collection of 236 poems spread over 200 pages. Except for the last 42 unpublished poems, the rest have been taken from ten poetry books, which were published between 1982 and 2016. Those ten published books are *When Grief Rains* (1982), *The Broken Rhythms* (1987), *The Fleeting Bubbles* (1989), *Melting Melodies* (1994), *Pensive Memories* (2005), *Gliding Ripples* (2008), *Echoes* (2012), *Quest for Peace* (2013), *Golden Veil* (2016) and *Thousand Haiku Pearls* (2016).

This book begins with Prof. Reddy's first collection of poems *When Grief Rains* (1982) from which eighteen selected poems are included here.

The title poem "When Grief Rains" expresses the core theme of this group of poems. Let me quote from the beautiful poem:

> When gales of sorrow
> wreck my surging spirit,
> misery storms my being,
> and grief rains incessantly
> I wish to drench myself,
> depart from these ills
> and enter the pores of the earth
> with drops of rain that seep.

Thus pent up, suppressed emotions express themselves in a rain of grieving poetry. Dr. Ramesh Chandra Mukhopadhyaya, in his research paper "T. V. Reddy's *When Grief Rains*: A Poetic Journey from Dystopia to Utopia," evaluates the book thus: "In fine we could describe *When Grief Rains* as a thrilling journey from distress to recovery and from dystopia to utopia. The sights and sounds of the paradise upon earth sink deep in the poet's being to flash upon his inward eye when he is faced with trauma engendered by the civilised society" (*The Poetic Art of T. V. Reddy: New Perspectives* 85).

It is followed by fifteen selected poems of Dr. Reddy's second collection of poems *The Broken Rhythms* (1987). The poems depict the plight of human beings, their miseries and obstacles that break the rhythm of happy life. Thereafter we find his next collection *The Fleeting Bubbles* (1989) from which sixteen poems are selected. The theme of the poems in this group is the transitory joy of human life. It is followed by nineteen selected poems of *Melting Melodies* (1994). The poet expresses his anger at the exploitation and neglect of the rural people by the politicians and administrators. Dr. Reddy also attacks the realm of education and the centres of higher learning which are getting degenerated. There are also excellent romantic poems in this group.

It is now followed by eighteen selected poems of *Pensive Memories* (2005). Personal experiences and touching events of Prof. Reddy's simple life are the main themes of these poems. The grief at the loss of the poet's dear wife gave birth to a few wonderful elegiac poems in this group. It is worth quoting what Dr. P. Suneetha wrote in her critical paper "The Poetic Art of T V Reddy: 'Regional Poet Par Excellence'": "The poet tries to unburden his heart, overloaded with grief over the loss of his spouse. It begins with a short poem 'A Lone Bird' where the poet is a lone bird after the exit of his spouse. This finds its fullest expression in the lengthy poem 'To My Other Half' which runs into thirteen ten-lined stanzas where each stanza is loaded with high intensity of grief:

Like a dream, like a wave you came
entwined my life like a lush creeper
lifted my soul to dizzy heights of rapture
warmly opened the doors of Elysium
and filled my life with heavenly joys
But what have you left me now?
Ashes of your pyre that consume my heart
Tender haunting melodic memories
Why have you done like this
Why have you left me alone in tears?

"This long poem stands out as unique and distinct, exhibiting the poet's everlasting love for his dear departed wife in these days of dwindling human sentiments and strained marital relationships" (*The Poetic Art of T. V. Reddy: New Perspectives* 31).

Thereafter we find thirty poems selected from *Gliding Ripples* (2008). Social, philosophical and individual concerns are the main themes in this group. Forty-five poems from the book *Echoes* (2012) are reprinted here. We listen to poems bearing the unfading echoes of eternal ethics among these selections. Dr. K. Rajani in her paper, "Echoes of Ethics in Dr. T. V. Reddy's *Echoes*" remarks that

"...among modern poets in Indian English, T. V. Reddy shines with his ceaseless effort in spreading the light of ethics in the society with his untiring crusade on corruption and degeneration of basic human values and moral standards in every walk of society. He is at once a poet of high calibre and a social reformer with a strong commitment to bring a healthy change in the society by strengthening the fibre of morality in the society in general" (*The Poetic Art of T. V. Reddy: New Perspectives* 328).

Now we are introduced to his next work *Quest for Peace* (2013) which is written as a minor social epic by Prof. T. V. Reddy. It is perhaps his magnum opus, reflecting the systematic deterioration of moral values. In seven sections, he presents the restless life of modern man. It is a rhymed poem and the rhyming patterns are like ABAB, AABB or ABBA, used in a mixed way. Prof. Kavitha Gopalakrishnan, in her paper "Nature of 'Nature': Reading the Nature/Culture Dichotomy in T. Vasudeva Reddy's *Quest for Peace,*" analyses the sections thus:

"The first section introduces the general theme of the loss of human values and the rampant corruption with the increasing growth of urban culture. The second section presents a bleak future as the people in power utilize/misutilize power much to nature's chagrin. The third section bemoans the satanic market values that govern people's actions. The fourth section says that we have given our peace in exchange for the triumphs we gain through corruption and exploitation. The fifth section gives a comparative understanding by juxtaposing past and present worlds. The sixth mocks man's rat race. The last section emphasises on the issue at hand and suggests few recommendations" (*The Poetic Art of T. V. Reddy: New Perspectives* 223).

Thirty two poems from *Golden Veil* (2016) now appear in this book. Let me borrow Prof. C. R. Visweswara Rao's words from his research article, "Veils Unveiled: T. V. Reddy's *Golden Veil: A Collection of Poems*":

"While many poems capture common human tendencies and susceptibilities, vanities and vagaries with a sharp realist eye, there are some that move on to the dramatization of a grander perspective of eternity intruding into time to seek to redeem it of its ravages" (*The Poetic Art of T. V. Reddy: New Perspectives* 42).

Golden Veil is followed by *Thousand Haiku Pearls* (2016) from which selected haiku are incorporated in this book. Various forms of unethical acts prevalent in society, and how they breed a hybrid culture, is one of the main themes of Prof. Reddy's haiku. Burning issues of society like poverty, starvation, unemployment, deprivations, loneliness, discrimination, etc., and celebration of nature are beautifully portrayed in these haiku.

This remarkable book comes to a meaningful end with the inclusion of forty-two unpublished poems of Dr. Reddy. Most of these poems are thought-provoking and their inner content stirs our hearts and disturbs many complacent minds and awakens us from torpor. The first poem 'Our Race' is a power-packed one capable of awakening a race lying in passivity and it is charged with vigour and vitality. Another poem 'Beneath the Colour', for instance, is without any doubt an inspiring one with its progressive ideas and universal truth. All these poems are excellent poems with sparkling thought, illuminating messages and profound values and some of them are rhymed and musical with melodic beauty.

Constraints of time and space compel me to wind up my foreword. Let me conclude by reinstating my opinion that this book, *T. V. Reddy's Poetry—The Pulse of Life: Essential Readings* will remain a milestone in the poetic career of Prof. Reddy, and conquer the minds of poetry lovers all over the world. It will enlighten and entertain the minds of young and old, and will be a treasure to any bookshelf or library.

—**Dr. K. V. Dominic**
(English poet, short story writer, critic and editor)

Introduction

This work *Essential Readings* is a representative collection of the poetry of T.V. Reddy, a luminous star shining in Indian English poetry. His poetry is a pleasant blend of the traditional and the modern, the realistic and the romantic, the symbolic and the imagist, the urban and the rural, satirical and lyrical streams of poetry. When Indian English poetry in the eighties of the last century was languishing for quality T.V. Reddy emerged as a potential signature with his quality-oriented poetry in English in India and he breathed into it both the throbbing life and melody with its rare lyrical charm. Poems, spread over eleven volumes till now, from his first poetry work (1982) till the recent one (2017) spell out the sustaining progress and quality of his poetry which makes Prof. Reddy an outstanding poet of the modern times.

His poems cover a wide thematic pattern ranging from the remote village to the global level, a bewildering blend of rural and global life. Whoever wishes to have a glimpse of the reality of the Indian rural scenario and see the struggles and sufferings of poor farmers can go through the poems of T.V. Reddy. It is not an exaggeration to say that very few poets can reach the lyrical heights he has scaled and his invincible talent in the creation of the melodic line is manifest in all his poems. His *Quest for Peace*, an artistic product as well as a realistic cross-section of the existing ethical, economic and political situation all over the world, is a poem of rare quality and stark beauty with the musical beat of its rhyme and indeed it is a social epic in miniature.

Themes of his recent poems in *Echoes* and *Golden Veil* stretch from India to the USA and the Central Park in New York becomes the centre of attraction while the Hudson river, Fall colours and Lurai Caves too find their place along with the ancient Fort and Palace of his native area in India besides other prominent places such as Thousand Pillars and Mahabalipuram in South India, Varanasi in the North, Badrinath Temple in the Himalayas and Amarnath Cave in Kashmir. A reading of the *Essential Readings* proves extremely fruitful in seeing the priceless literary treasures hidden in the poetry of Dr. T.V. Reddy who is second to none in the field of World poetry.

When Grief Rains
(N Delhi, Samkaleen Pubs., 1982)

The Balmy Smile

A drop of rain
frays the furious sun;
A ray of the sun
caresses the frozen snow;
A spark of fire
wakes up the slumbering coal;
The guffaw of breeze
soothes the sultry land;
Flowery fragrance
lulls the stench to sleep;
The smile of a child
laces the clouds of gloom.

Sweet Scar

I thought:
sweetness erupts when we peel
and vacillate in blissful union.
Now I realize:
When that dream dissolves,
the pensive memory of the scar
on the wounded heart
is tastier than those spasms.
I don't wish to brush it off
by union with another
or by painting a reunion !

The Sparrow

It picked in zeal
the veins of a leaf,
wove a nest
with its beak

to hatch the eggs.
The ominous crow
invaded the grassy womb
and the lone sparrow fled
away from the vacuous nest.
A flutter of waiting wings:
the sky squawked in requiem.

The East

Look at the east:
still it is dark.
An invisible hand
has lit the vaulted pyre;
from the grey ashes of yesterday
rise the rays of sunlight
phoenix-like.

Gray Hair

An abhorring sight:
Your repelling reflection,
A silvery line on the temple
To be slain with razor's edge.
I curse your accused shadow,
The precursor of the eerie end.
I shall uproot you with a spade
From the tawny beard.
Do you still dare mock at me?
I dread thy yet unborn progeny
And flee from the reflected agony.

Patience

Have patience:
That is your armour.
Even when your patience is tired
don't become impatient,
you then become a beast.
Be firm and tolerant as the temple tower
That blesses the mindless fanatics
and stands up to the stormy winds.
Tempests often corrode
the carvings of the tower – not of Babel –

Yet they smile at and kiss the gales
And shelter the poor with open gates;
Thousands of noisy Lilliputians enter.
Though the murky clouds obscure its peak
Like a potent warrior it emerges unbeaten;
It is a moral giant preaching values,
A standing monument of patience.
Be patient or become a patient:
Make an ashram or an asylum.
The prescription has been patented.

Potent Drop

The earth is round,
like a pointless top it revolves.
The glass of liquor
elevates me to the skies;
woe, the timid foe, flies
out of the microbial bubbles.
The place is full of wasps
and venomous asps
that suck my beleaguered blood
with the mortal sting.
Why should I waste
my short span of life
by thinking of those
that laugh at my sorrows
and wish to toll my knell?
I am in the lotus island;
The power of the drop wanes,
the divine reverie fades,
and scenes of reality serenade.

Civilization

Civilization has grown
with the speed of a snail;
its spread is as thick
as the Amazonian forest
full of prickly thorns,
venomous snakes
and dreadful shadows.
The shell of sophistication

conceals its foul interior,
worse than an addled egg.
Craze for naked beauty
gives a boost to the nude,
a return to the primitive.
The age has specialized
in each sucking other's blood.
The day is not far off
when the monstrous python
of greed, deceit and lust
would devour the society
at its zenith of civilization
swiftly tolling the knell
to the nutritious values of human life.

Futility

The Nothingness around me gapes and gasps;
It hardly breathes – a baneful breeze!
I hear lying still on the hard mat
The dinning sound of the futile struggle.
With heavy and burning eyes I am awake.
Robbed of my only wealth of dreams
I can neither sleep nor see.
My hushed speech makes even my shadow blush;
I cannot speak to any one but my own negative.
I plead before the shapeless shades
Of the pervading futility and sterility;
My attempt to smile becomes abortive;
So as to recover my confidence
I look into the time mirror:
Alas! It already broke into hundred odd pieces;
Million images run away from me in dread,
A vast tract of vacuum stretches
To the farthest edge of futility.
Disturbed by hazy memories of the past
Like wisps of receding cigarette smoke
That blurs the keen camera of vision
Life recedes into the vast barren expanse.

When Grief Rains

When gales of sorrow

wreck my surging spirit,
misery storms my being,
and grief rains incessantly
I wish to drench myself,
depart from these ills
and enter the pores of the earth
with drops of rain that seep.
Still somewhere in me
a dim desire creeps unawares
to possess the instinctive mackintosh.

A Pinch of Faith

Around a pinch of faith
an army of dark bodies
roll in waves of countless doubts;
suspicions, uncertainties and fears
are on their frail minds.
Doubt spreads the shroud
of death on the living;
yet faith twinkles.
Legions live after death
on the tomb of profit
satiating their lustful hunger
by buying bodies with fake notes,
quenching their inordinate thirst
with the blood of the weak and meek,
spreading the shining spoils
on the tomb of boundless lust,
while they share their baneful booty
in the blessed burial ground;
the raucous rays of their eyes
burn the culture of the ages,
illumine the livid light of the pyre;
the departed sneeze at the Lethe
sniffing a stifling pinch of faith.

Thirsty Field

Breaking the series
of deafening thunders,
tearing the continuous
line of lightnings,

drops of rain traversed
through the darkened sky
and touched the thirsty fields.
Hardly they entered
the countless cracks,
the period proved abortive.
Jilted by crafty clouds
the sun-burnt crop looked
like a dissected corpse
on the post-mortem table.

Transience

All the land under the warm sun
seems ruefully inadequate
for the man who feels eternal.
And when the end seizes him,
he has no voice to claim
even a mere six by two.
The body, full of punctures,
in its long tedious journey
succumbs to inevitable decay,
searches for solace in the dark cradle.
There is nothing to gain in life
or anything to lose in death;
the former is robbed of its lively spell,
the latter of its deadly shell.
Triumph and sloth have their common day,
beauty and beggary merge in clay;
Great deeds are writ in water,
All glories lead only to dust.

Realisation

I climbed half the hill
and in fact I do not know
how I reached it at all.
Life's major part was spent
without my being aware of it;
a vague and obscure career
full of futility – a waste land,
a dreary desert full of sand.
I recalled I was a boy yesterday

playing with others by the river.
I see now on the horizon
a vast stretch of silent cemetery.
My hair is as white as cotton;
I resign myself to my finale
and wait for the inevitable moment
with a foot firmly planted
inside the last resting place.

The Wood is Calm

The wood is calm, the trees are erect;
The leaves form a layered roof near the heavens;
The fruits are hanging like suspended stars
From the leafy sky, bluish green and breathless.
Robust and green is the woody hill,
Up there the climate is healthy and chill;
Water crystal clear from above the hill
Flows with sweet and soothing thrill.
Slides the ravishing stream among the rocks,
Swings swiftly into serpentine tracks,
And again rolls into slackened cracks
Producing melody on the greeting rocks.
In the ravine a rock is seen, steep and huge,
Plain and white glittering like silver:
And on it lies a root firm but large
And travels to the bottom of the stone.
Down the water falls from the top of the hill,
Along the root on the breast of the rock
Runs in smiles, all the pits it tries to fill,
And again slides in joy on stone and stock.
It is a paradise with such a sylvan scene,
We went on a picnic to this woody theatre;
Ineffable was our joy at the vernal scene serene
A healing balm it was for our clouded spirits later.

The Lake at Night

The lake is calm, quiet is the night,
Yonder the moon, an orb of cheese,
Blanches the earth with her milk-white fleece
And is bright with a flood of tender light.
Like the face of a sleeping babe the water is still

Slumbering at the firm foot of the verdurous hill.
It is clear as crystal with colour azure
Shines like a vast sheet of sheeny silver pure.
Oh! Behold beneath the sluggish surface
Of water deep and drowsy with a wizard's face!
The sky is inverted with the moon and the milky way,
The blinking stars dance deep in the tranquil bay.
The earthen bank stands like a girdle of gold
Around the waist of the bride from ages old
Or like a bold defiant lover in his amorous arms
Hugging the sprightly damsel full of charms
Printing her quivering lips with kisses serene
Pressing her swelling breasts in raptures keen.
On either side of the circuitous bank
The lush growth of plants adorn the tank
Tall spreading trees with many a pendent nest
Provide rich green shelter for birds to rest;
Ghostly flowers blue, white and violet
Dance eerily to please the high-browed Hecate;
The rippling tides touch the majestic hill,
Stray birds make their tired strains shrill,
The distracting human noise is dead,
The foolish frogs croak all night instead;
The sphere seems to be a cold corpse sombre
With the blue dome above as the sepulchre;
I feel the pensive melody of the gloomy globe
In air, water and dust shrouded in sable robe.

My Soul's Agony

Forgive me, an unworthy self, my love!
Far away I worship you in my pupil
My heart doesn't beat without your thought
Distance deprives me of your tender touch
It trebles my soul's dumb agony
My heart burns with gratitude
Yet I cannot even comfort you
Me alive, I am indeed dead to you
You are there alone – a dove in a nest
You clung to me like a tender ivy
You nursed, freed and befriended me
You opened to me the doors of Elysium
I did not know. A transcendental touch!

What did I to you? An unkind wretch!
I measured you with sugar spoons
And coffee cups. A cruel arithmetic!
I am afar, for me, for you and for us
Yet here I am none to me
Eating in the hotel a few crumbs
fried in the penitential fire;
When shall I come to you to place
the remnants of my heart at your feet?
A tedious journey full of regrets
on the soil through the dust to dust.

The Last Journey

The haughty human frame is inflexible
The dainty skin abruptly insensitive
The lusty lips meekly cold and wry
Shining pearls turn strangely rigid
Fastidious tongue is hard
Hugging hands are strangely frozen.
Gone are the skills of the bard
Fingers yield to cruel stillness.
Legs that climbed many a cliff
Like logs of wood are stiff,
The foot that spurned the weak
Before the Higher Order is meek;
The voice that once thundered is silent
Threat or appeal dissolves for ever
The daring heart is an addled egg
Wily whispers enter his ears never.
The mighty mind that hatched
Many a sordid scheme is sterile,
The expressive eyes that sent
Smiles and shudders now beguile.
In a far off land strange and unknown
On the putrid pavement of a busy street
Lies the rigid frame of a man unknown
Covered with cloth, an inert candle by his side.
Passers-by throw coins on the soiled cloth
To meet the expenses for his last journey.
When this mortal flame is put out
We do not know where we end up.

The Broken Rhythms
(Madras, Poets Press India, 1987)

Thousand Pillars*

They cry in mute agony
With their limbs mutilated;
The sight seres the welled eyes
And pierces the chilled spine
With thousand swords;
The inspired sculptors
Who chiselled delicate figures
And breathed life into the rock
Decayed into dust ages ago;
The potent royal patrons
Fell into oblivion in disgrace;
Still the pillars outlive the pillage
And cast a pensive spell
With their intricate patterns;
The beheaded heads gnaw our hearts,
The distant madanikas** in varies poses
Enchant the eye and enslave the soul;
The speck of every tiny wreck
Is an indelible blot on humanity,
The negation of any noble creed;
While divinity throbs the stone
The ruins preach the self-same gospel.

Note:
* The famous temple near Warangal (in A.P) constructed by the Kakatiya Kings in 12C.A.D.; destroyed in early 14C by the army of Alauddin Khilji.

** Refers to the ravishing sculpture in the Ramappa Temple, constructed by the Kakatiya Kings in 1213 A.D. (situated at a distance of 70 K.Ms. from Warangal, A.P.)

Fortune-Teller

To touch the tip of Fortune's toe
even in dream is a bliss in woe:
The bearded one, wise and old,
with vermilion on the forehead,
armoured well with amulets,
sits beneath the banyan tree
with a little cage, a bundle of palm leaves
and a pack of cards by his side;
His green winged captive, a parrot,
is his friend, philosopher and guide;
the pedestrian, a fond wiseacre,
comes and pays a coin,
the crimson-beaked bird
picks a card with wonted skill
and gives it to the wise master
who discloses his lucky dip.
The client goes gratified
with winged hope at his door
unaware of the dear duplicity;
the bird blind to his fortune
of flying freedom in the green sky
decides the destinies of others;
the fortune teller
doubtful of his morrow's fortunes
counts his easy earnings on the canvas.

The Milky Way

On the shores of Aegean sea
ages ago Sophocles watched
the hoary sound of weird waves
and the vast dark expanse, a crux;
Bulwark of brightest brains
is hewn into legion of shreds
as it gazes at the milky way
that keeps darkling souls at bay.
The musing mind like summer tyre
may tire and burst in friction
it hardly sees a fraction of truth.
The genii of this wondrous sphere
with the power of all their years

dare not touch the rim of cosmos
nor traverse a wink of light year;
The animating frame of universe
with all the stars as eyes
may shrink to see the creation,
lungs of planets may sigh with T.B.
Vedic Rishis cracked their brains,
retreated in despair to forests
and spent their breath in penance.

The Train

The belch of suffocating smoke,
as thick as the breath of the coalminer,
the huge mouth of demoniac engine
emitted forth with a deafening roar.
Numerous people from far and near
of various climes, customs and creeds
with their diverse distracting tongues
made the compartment a tiny nation;
bustle and whistle gave it a queer life.
Sitting near the open window
I thought it is the earth that moves,
it is true, the palm trees race fast,
The child sees it, the sage said it;
The race slowed and ceased.
Some got down and a few entered;
faces that shone became faint and dim,
tears of joy and sorrow became one,
smiles that sprang receded to shores.
Thinning crowds faded into shadows,
the Babel and grave quietness merged.
Men may come and men may go,
grey heads die and babes tumble
but the train translates on parallel rails
as time sprints forever on invisible tracks.

A Leper

A blemished mass wrapped in rags
that hardly cover the reeking ruins
shivers as a vibrating tuning fork.
A voice emerges, a faint echo

from the hollow deep haunting,
begging alms from every pedestrian.
A semblance of a seeming hand
mutilated by some higher power
stretches a plate in grateful bow
some pity his gnawing fate,
a few spit at his odious sight;
a dog empties the remnants of a leaf,
passes by in cherubic contentment
while the leper reels in living death
that flees from him in dread.

Pensive Farmer

The pensive farmer plods his way
with his feet bare and sore,
his pair of famished bulls
limping desperately in front of him,
bundle of hay on his heaving head,
to perform his duty of reaching home
where his spouse, ordained to share his lot,
struggles hard before the hostile hearth
to cook a morsel of rice with a few twigs.
He comes at last, does his routine,
bathes and stretches his aching body
on the pricking mat spread on stone.
They share the ordeal of taking rice
with tamarind chutney and butter milk;
Nearby the bulls reluctantly bite the hay
and lie on the ground beneath the tree;
Reconciled to their gloomy destiny
and still finding fault with their creation
they proceed to the ritual of procreation;
drained and tired they cough
that echoes in empty clay barrels
their only inheritance to store the grain;
All the village is quite as the graveyard,
veil of darkness concealing its flaccid face.

Swamiji

He was clad in ochre-coloured robes
That touched his toe and sailed with wind,
His fingers shone with rings of gold
His wrist radiant with an imported watch;
They say His Holiness, feet, soft and gentle,
Would never touch this mortal dust;
It is true, he got down from a Cadillac
From amid a bevy of choicest beauties
That vied with each other to gratify him.
Millionaires came and touched his feet,
His savings swelled like elephantiasis;
Swamiji spoke on Man, God and Soul,
The potter and clay were his easy victims;
The stunned audience were all ears.
They all praised his spiritualism and simplicity
For he ate only apples, cashew nuts and dried grapes,
Drank pure milk and juice brought by fair-sex;
His holiness left, leaving his fragrance behind.

Cosmic Love

With my arms
spread to the distant skies
I wish to embrace you;
With my face
touching the heavens
I wish to kiss your ruby lips
the portals of rosy bliss;
With my feet
rooted to the earth
I wish to go with you
and find our peace
with our cosmic love
in the other world.

My Fair Lady

If
You are a blossoming flower
        let me be the bee
        that sucks its honey;
You are a tender creeper

      let me be thy prop
        that sustains you forever;
You are a divine flute
      let me be its sweet strain
      that gives life to the organ;
You are an Ajanta fresco
      let me be the mirror in thy hand
      to reflect thy delicate face;
You are a Belur sculpture
      let me be the ornament
      that makes your feet celestial;
Let me be thy serene breath
and thy constant shadow.

Between the Lines

Our excited hearts throbbed
and twittered in tuneful unison,
dreamy eyes half-closed in charm
vibrating lips quivered
and fondly nibbled the nipples,
divine drops of nectar
blessed the caressing tongue,
hissing breath gasped,
hands surveyed the sketch
grasped the pointed peaks
of the two peerless pagodas
and pressed the fleshy pillows;
fingers frantically probed
between the luscious lines
for the red rose in wilderness,
bodies welded by electric arc
coiled and twisted in rapture –
dynamics and hydrostatics;
doors of Elysium opened
lifting us to starry realms,
legion starts twinkled,
blinding lightning flicked –
flickering wick in embers
flood of dull darkness
dim delight in deluge;
pallid calm followed
the storm in a tea cup.

The Gipsy Woman

With a basket
Woven of palm leaves
Balanced meticulously
On the dishevelled head
She walks along the street
Treading the scorching ground
With her bare tripping feet;
Her silver anklets and bracelets
Vie in arresting heaviness.
Her broad bangles jingle,
Garlands of patches on her sari
Host the molesting sun,
Pieces of mirror sewn on her dress
Reflect the piercing rays
While her arms move
In tune with her slender waist;
She cries with an assured voice –
"I can tell your fortunes –
hear my '*sode*'*, know thy future
sode amma *sode*, hear my *sode*",
pauses at each door-step
feels the palm of rustic maid
with her wondrous wand
and discloses the pages of fate
in words of musical cadence
and earns palmfuls of rice;
By telling sweet and sensible lies,
interspersed with generalizations,
she fills the hearts of maids
with honeyed thoughts;
they gain a parcel of sweet dreams
while she her remorseless morsel.
*Telugu word used by gipsy women for telling the past, present and
future.

The Typist Girl

Tick ... ... .tick tick... ... ... tick
Letters vomit on the carbon
through the frail and sickly ribbon;
the fair and flowery fingers

press the lettered buttons
with mechanical speed
and struggle to tame
the old and defiant type-writer;
The incessant sound
conceals the unrealized dreams
of an unfulfilled heart
and echoes its mechanical beat;
The two down cast eyes gasp
to escape the peeping prying
prowling lascivious looks;
the boss and the menial alike
eye at her in intent gaze
ready to rob the flower
of its chaste fragrance.
Wearied of her thorny journey
her two minds merge into one
as she decides with a dry smile
to spread her youthful beauty
like a red carpet to the M.D.,
who draining a bottle of whisky
tempts her with a lure and a leer,
and ensures her rise in status
before the sun-rise.

The Report

The wooden door was locked outside
but he was found still inside the cottage
facing the temple tower, a skyscraper;
he was alone, his mate had gone
long before it was sadly found
and the shady scene was seen;
The report of the post-mortem said –
heart failure of a man, sober and staid;
the police enquiry conveyed to the press –
Manager of a private company
a gentleman of normal degree
who pleased his boss and the workers;
confidentials were enviable
credentials were acceptable.
That morn the bundles of currency
he dumped in the divine Hundi

was a loud proof of his faith in God;
an angel at home, an asset to the firm;
His love for his wife was beyond doubt,
recently he brought her a diamond necklace
that shone in every function of the town;
He was a civilized man far from want,
he had a gas stove, a T.V and a scooter
he made a sweet home and a bright firm;
he fathered only a son and a daughter,
got incentives for Family Planning,
his talent averted strikes and lock-outs;
He came to the Hills for a change,
last night in the dead hour
the creeping errand boy espied him
exchanging irate looks of envy,
he did not wake up to see the day;
Is it a foul play or a fair end?
Was he good? A meaningless query;
Report is valid; peace be to the manes.

Sacred Soil

In this ancient land
of glorious cultures
omnivorous vultures
reign supreme;
once a crucible of religions
is transformed into
a cubicle of callous creeds
blind, dark and dubious;
Long ago Buddha's soul fled
to foreign shores in dread
Gandhi's trembling ghost
is chased from pillar to post
till it bleeds and recedes;
The nascent vigour
of our coffee culture
mars like a rugged bear
the green Harappan glory;
the shallow slogans
of our elected leaders
make Hampi ruins grieve;
In this sacred soil

of conflicting isms
that reflect cataclysms
and political prisms
that refract nefarious hues
much is talked about
in corrupt Assembly halls
and thatched tea stalls;
corpulent ministers
and famished minstrels
sing Subhash's heroism
and parade his martial portrait
whose spirit sheds
a flood of invisible tears
that form a new Ganga;
righteous action is scarce
as sugar or cement,
it is a rare species
nearing total extinction,
The tidal wave of caste,
colour and community
makes a weird dance
and tolls the knell of unity;
Unity in diversity
is a fascinating word
like seeking water
in a summer mirage;
Still after scorching summer
can rains evade for ever
with elusive clouds?

A Poem

A poem now a days
is only to be read
and to break one's head
in several ways
with the so-called hammer
of stammered words,
dry hard nuts
not to be bitten
but to be thrown
as a heap of litter
in the dust bin,

a vanishing cream
that leaves an uneasy dream;
if it can't give
a semblance of pleasure
in our scanty leisure,
it is, no doubt, a curse
to browse through a verse;
if it is an exercise
and versified algebra
to a muddled mind,
sure, it is a prosaic one
that sends one seek shelter
one day in an asylum;
all the three tenses need
a line that refreshes the mind,
an ennobling line serene,
the true taste of Hippocrene.

The Fleeting Bubbles
(Madras, Poets Press India, 1989)

Women of the Village

Beneath the pale peepal tree
by the fast drying pond
in that double roasted hamlet
women stand like expiring candles
Passively they fill
their empty earthen pots
bending like famished cattle
that drain water to the lees
The clear water moves
in concentric circles
like their day dreams
snaky visages in water
weaving desires in the plaits
of their cobra-long hair
they carry pots of sweat
Covering staring breasts
with their sari-ends
they turn homeward with pitchers
and wait for their men
with flickers in their eyes.

The Indian Bride

Amid vaunting faces of kith and kin
concentric circles of friends
she is alone in solitude
sitting by the winking groom.
As mute as an adorned idol
in an overcrowded temple
she sits depressed, a mind agitated.
Dressed in gold-laced Kanchi silk sari
adorned with stone-studded jewellery
she looks like a bedecked doll in a show case

or a vanishing species in a zoo.
The rising waves and stormy gales
of the Bay of Bengal pale here.
The contours of her heaving bosom
draw the E.C.G of her uncertain fate
to be shared with an unseen face;
Beneath the surging smiles of guests
pomp and pageantry, glitter and feast
flows the eddying stream of her parent's tears;
the Purohit performs the rites by Agni
while they see the borrowed currency in flames;
wedding music charms her heart
though drained by traditional ills;
Hopes fill her mind like summer showers
soon fears settle like monsoon clouds;
The triple knot of 'thali' around her neck
shining symbol of new bondage
mocks at the thrice-cursed bride.
Having bought the groom in auction
as cattle dealers buy their lusty bulls,.
she is content to be his slave
ready to play to his whimsical tunes
and pay heavily for the dear prize.

The Hospital

The case remains the same
No change in patient's condition –
the chief doctor burning a cigar
with decades of decadent experience
gives his Delphic oracle
after a fortnight's senseless stay;
in the I.C.U. of the Emergency ward
all tests are conducted
diagnosis seems to reach its destination;
treatment continues round the clock
for the probable disease,
still an enigma baffling their brains,
Nine-tenths of their knowledge
assumes it to be a type of tetanus
while the remainder suggests meningitis
still a fraction roams in ambiguity
a larger cloudy canvas, the nebula;

some nurses treat like real sisters
while their seniors in white robes
behave like white elephants,
a few new-hatched doctors
wear airs pruning their plumage
like young Chanticleers
winking at the studious steths;
The priest prays at bed-side
the Great Healer for speedy recovery;
On the road of trial and error
one quizzical drug cures the patient
and drowns the profession in wonder;
At last they pride themselves
when the disease, the vanquished victor,
walks majestically with another prey
in search of a fresh contract.

A Forlorn Soul

My heart groans
I see myself burnt unmercifully
on the pyre of my wounded feelings
which are crushed between the grinding jaws
of my kith and kin, too selfish,
deprived of sympathy.
Liver thus roasted with gridiron
on the sparks of flaming greed
appeases their fastidious tongues.
My eyes are gnawed by aberration,
blindness alone is divine sight;
timid tears sink inside their refuge
and dare not show their fluid face,
the hand that served as a prop
is now shunned as a contagion;
with all my people around
I am alone, a forsaken man
a lone one with a desperate will
to drift the rudderless course
to safe shores – a vain bid;
perchance it is not worth the times,
people strangle my forlorn soul
and toll my knell in triumph.

The Cry

From the death cry
that pierced the heart
when the hunting arrow
nipped the neck of a dove
emerged the immortal epic;
From the agonized cry
of the oppressed brethren
crushed between the grinding
jaws of the greedy rich
ushers the drum of dissent
and the clarion of insurrection;
springs the volley of thunder bolts
and rise the potent sparks of revolt
whose flames kiss the sky
and reduce life to ashes
from which rises phoenix.

Tide

Tide
Stop thy pride
and foarning ride
Beware
of your momentous fall
before your heart breaks
at the solid shores.

The Dark Valley

My heart bleeds, my torpid brain sizzles,
A pigmy cauldron to hold the seething riddles;
The way that used to be smooth and clear
Is now strewn with blazing sparks of fire;
The hair pricks the skull with pins of pains,
Oh! the bitter gall of woes flows in veins;
It saps the thought and fells the edge.
To face the shafts of life was once my pledge,
Alas! Meek suffering has become my badge;
To cross the maze of misery there is no bridge,
Too many are the troubles to solve or to abridge,
Too tired of clambering up the craggy ridge
I faint and fall headlong into the vale of night,

In vain I grope in the dark to catch a beam of light.

My Soul in Exile

Don't quit, my love,
Without you
why should I live
why should I be here
and lose my identity
in this prison of a world?
How long shall I hide
this bitter potion
in my galled throat
and produce melodies
in uneasy ecstasy
with my soul in exile?
If your voice is still,
my throat doesn't move;
with glottis in pensive arrest,
tongue becomes mute,
pen, dry and lifeless;
Don't quit, be with me,
my prop in stress and strain,
let us sail or sink together.

Old Woman

'Please give me alms, O charitable one!
I am an old woman with help from none' –
a familiar voice that breeds no contempt;
she lived on alms and lived near the temple gate.
Her hair as gloomily grey as clusters of snakes,
unkempt, uncombed and untouched by oil,
Her nails often scratched her scalp
and brutally killed lice that lived there long;
Stitches on her sari outnumbered her wrinkles,
Her arms were bare with blistering boils
Her face, brow and breasts were all wrinkles;
without a third leg her feet scarcely moved
Her eyes struggled to see with fading power
Her fingers feebly counted the coins in her bowl
A faint smile shone on her pensive face
she didn't want more than her stomach's fill

Nor did she espy the stealthy eyes of her neighbour;
Still her prayers to God had a single wish
She implored Him to take her to His world sooner
She spent her laborious days for deliverance
with a beam of hope striking her heavy bosom.
The lone God was made a captive in His temple,
the lone woman a victim to world's caprices;
The Swamiji saw her on his way, spat at her
And went in fury for his ill-luck to see her first.
Long back she resolved to have neither eyes nor ears,
She sat on the hard but hospitable stone for decades;
A statue of tolerance fed on harsh ignominy
A haunting figure with a soul wrung in agony.

The Corn Reaper

Under the scorching sun
in the ripened paddy field
she reaped the fallen crop
with the multi-toothed sickle,
sweat flowed drop by drop
from her care-worn brow;
the lustful eyes of the land-lord
fell on her heaving bosom;
unaware of other's eyebrow
she cut the corn patiently
sitting like a flower under the foot
thinking of her wailing child at home
and of the volley of blows on her back
given last night by her drunken lord.

The Teacher

At last the gloomy day has come
After decades of devoted duty
The mind that struggled
To transmit light to dark cavities
Is now destined to quiet decay;
Retirement from the chair or the stage
is a certainty – a worn-out truth;
it is a pensive reflection;
Still man wishes time to be still
and if possible to retrace its course.

But his exit creates a vacuum.
The brassy voice is now alien to the hall
The echo haunts the mind in its fall
The receding step touches the heart.
The painter paints his masterpiece
and sculptor carves his statue,
full of life they are deaf and dumb;
but a teacher breathes life into living logs
and moulds the erring minds
into worthy beings of the species.
His guiding spirit is the pupil of his pupils
He transforms baser metal and ennobles
with the alchemic power of his word;
Gift of the gab is his magic wand
that does miracles and brings metamorphosis;
Teacher gives a fresh lease of life
and breathes meaning into existence;
If the Almighty creates, he re creates
and transforms the raw substance
into a refined one, rich and noble;
through ages he is like a candle
that burns and spreads light,
ignored and forgotten after its exit.

The Snake-Charmer

Squatting like a skinny skeleton
beneath a canopied tamarind tree
a lone sentinel amid a cluster of huts,
he poured breath into the gourd-pipe
which like a magic wand
spread its charm of music grand
that embosomed thrill and threat;
the old and the young gazed at
the charmer and the bamboo basket
He took off the lid restive
The cobra, the vanquished captive,
emerged like blind Samson
with a stony glitter in its lidless eyes
hissing in vain with vengeance
raising its dreaded hood
with all its mortal fangs removed;
it danced unawares in tune

with the uncanny music;
for all the risk he courted.

Democratic Lines

In this set-up of apparent democracy
a multi-purpose word of lip-service
a baneful breath and an abscess –
the greater the degree of hypocrisy
the stronger the asset to be a leader;
He is masses' matinee idol
the black marketeer or the broker
the racketeer or the gambler
an unruly student to whom
academic books are untouchables
or the cine actor rolling in black money
to whom sacrifice is a strange word –
anyone can become a leader;
He knows the trick of whipping passions
which he can trade to his ends
and encash the glamour to his success;
A wolf in ass's hide reigns
a hoarder in hermit's guise
strides with a load of lies
content with the soaring price
of leaves and loaves, meat and rice;
As simulation becomes his element
and cashew nuts his regular aliment
he is deaf to the people's ailment;
While masses groan under his vain promises
his relatives revel in ill-gotten wealth;
The elected leader leads his caste,
the self-styled saviour saves his kindred;
A term in chair insures his progeny
from want for generations many.
Exhorting others to sacrifice gold and cash,
he liberally parts with a pinch of sacred ash;
While oppressed people await elections
He hopes to win by buying voters
With money and arrack or with posters;
If a new man comes on democratic lines
Soon he starts the game on parallel lines.

The Mind

Mind is the laboratory
that discloses the laws of truth
amid illusions and speculations;
it solves the insoluble
when rightly directed
for the pursuit of truth
with infinite patience.
With the spark of spirituality
it is the seat of the super-conscious;
With good discipline
it adorns the inner life
strongly built
on the granite foundations
insoluble against the ages;
With the inner eye
on the everlasting and the eternal
it ignores the transitory lures;
Mind becomes rich
with an ennobling soul
the immutable image
of the Supreme Being.

The Kite

Behold yonder in the sky
the long-tailed eagle sailing
drawing brittle strength
from a rain-bow twig
and bonded life from a bundle of thread
a flimsy bridle to its vagaries;
It adorns the ethereal height
with its thrilling flight
from the earthly base
as an airy messenger of peace
borne aloft on the breezy palanquin;
It comes down or gets lost
with a break in the thread
or a dent in its square space
like the unrealized dreams
of the common man;
While the upward voyage

marks the soaring prices of the age
and the rising artificiality,
its steady descent embraces
a downward trend in values;
kite, fallen and torn on the hedge,
pensively recalls the wailing woman
molested on the sacred soil
by vultures alien to culture.

Lotus

Yonder in the pond
lotus smiles in serene joy
floating above waters
and invites to partake its bliss
and pick out pearls
from its leafy platter;
The unfolding petals
as many as the hurdles
that lie across life's journey
bloom like the blossoming soul;
it rises from the mud
but begets pure beauty
and spreads divine fragrance;
Likewise soul encapsuled in body
sheds slime and mortal coil,
soars to ethereal heights
and loses identity in the eternal.

Melting Melodies

(Madras, Poets Press India, 1994)

The Kalyani Dam

Near the golden rim
of the Western pagodas
the vanquished victor sets.
    Veiled by green foliage
    teak trees and tamarind trunks
    the thorny waters roar
    and rape the rocky bank;
    fiercely caressing
    the frigid stones
    seminal cataract gushes
    into rocky crevices
    of craggy cliffs.
The frenzied race
is arrested by the dam
that bridges the two hills
whose stony nipples
invite the starry clouds;
crystal waters become still
yawning its deep dark womb.
    Like a pregnant woman
    with terrible beauty
    the wearied waters glide.

Dharmasala

Thy soothing waves of breeze
    harbingers of peace and bliss
    greet the visitors with a kiss
Fatigue and fretful thoughts,
    alien elements here,
    flee to the peevish plains
Snow and the sun alike sprinkle
    cosily chill and cheerful smiles

     with an amber-tinted aura
The murmuring streams
     with perennial crystal flow
     throb the heart and arrest its beat
The range of high mountains
     with battalions of tall pines,
     wearied mountaineers
     resting while scaling the heights,
     pours its beauty into the pores of hearts
The steep and deep valleys all around
     seize the breath and make it free
     to gallop on the green carpet
     and hop in joy on the ascending
     green cascade of tea and corn fields
The place is quiet, leaves are still
even frogs seem to be in meditation
Night deep and still and undisturbed
save the melody of the dancing rills
There is majesty in its wild beauty
The place with the snow-clad peaks
of Dhawaldhara kissed by morning rays
looks like the peerless virgin beauty
of the coy Indian maid in milk white sari
that hides her heaving bosom
after her entrancing bridal bath.
While Siva and Buddha meditate here
Bhag Su Nag Valley, wide and deep,
an inverted cone of enchanting sweep
fills the mind with intense awe
inspires an increasing sense
of our littleness and nature's abundance –
dusty pins before might pines.
A tranquil place for lofty thoughts
an unearthly spot on the heights of earth
a *thapovan* for sages to meditate
The snowy peaks make the soul sublime
torrential rains enrich the creative springs
True to the name you preach
the shining value of eternal truth
and host the wearied pilgrims
in their march to the celestial summit
in diverse ways to reach the goal eternal.

The Fort*

It stands defenceless
Bare and bruised and deserted
a skeleton of a maimed and mangled soldier
wringing pity from flinty hearts
squeezing tears from glassy eyes
The mutilated massive entrance
of giant stone work with intricate designs
meekly greets from the land of the dead
to breathe the dry vapour of blood
while humble Hanuman for ages
stands with folded hands like a sage
with a plea to save the citadel
and the forgotten empire from oblivion
The impenetrable circuitous wall
atop the radiating crescent hill
stands pensive, detached and sublime,
reconciled to the fall of its patrons;
the moat once a purple pool of blood
is now transformed into a farm.
The eyes, two dry springs,
wish they had no light in them
to see the blasting heaps of ruins
of a hundred temples desecrated,
axed, wrecked and razed to the ground –
an act of sacrilege and wild savagery
that left no shadow of a bygone glory;
Amid the vast expanse of desolate ruins
fallen crowns and vanished sceptres
stands crest-fallen the majestic Raja Mahal
the wonder of the baffled modern architect
a living witness to the Royal permission
that sowed the seed for the white empire
the lone sentinel guarding unarmed
the barren stretch of invisible cemetery
of the Royal dynasties in dust
while the sweet crystal pearls
of the royal tank down the rocky hill
dance like princesses on the lotus leaves
to the unheard fragrant ditties
of the peerless petals of beauteous lotus;

The broken limbs of chiselled statues
that sapped the span of inspired sculptors
lie in the mortuary after heinous post-mortem;
Every piece of ruin, a marvel of art in stone,
carves a mute message, echoes a faded epic,
each tiny speck an iridescent luminous spark.

*Refers to Chandragiri Fort near Tirupati, A.P. The Raja Mahal was constructed in 1000 A.D., while the Fort during the period of the great Vijayanagar empire. Chandragiri became the capital of Vijayanagar kings after the ruin of Vijayanagar or Humpi in 1565 A.D. in late 16th and early 17th centuries.

The Taj

You stand on the banks of the Yamuna
like a haunting apparition in solid snow
in full fantastic magnificence
wrought by the force of Mulciber
and guarded by four towering sentinels
spreading lunar light on lunatic love.
Stamping your majestic feet on sweat
you enshrine the boundless love
in your solid stones and echoing hollows
fill the mind and soul with serene love;
All lust and carnal quest vanish,
Fabulous memory of a pensive tale
a marvel or chiselled elegy in marble
whose every stone echoes the epic of love.

The Toiling Woman

She breaks the rocks
and conquers the hill,
but at her Fortune mocks
and makes the moment still
as she bathes in the pool of sweat
to save her child from threat;
Though thin and weak
with her heart resolute as teak
she quells the defiant stone
with the hammer in her bone;
She lifts stones and bricks

with eyes full of wicks,
builds for others mansions and forts
to roll in foaming comforts;
All her sweat ensures her a hut
while her toil enthrones the lust.

The Village Girl

Twilight
sinking into dusk
a girl in pale brown
came to the stream
and gracefully filled her pot
with brownish water;
keeping the pot at the waist's curve
she balanced her lonely way
and carried the dusk away,
but her poor melting shadow
lingered long with ripples
in my mind's mellowed stream.

The Voyage of Life

This life
is a pensive path
of sweet memories
of eerie eclipses
melancholy reflections
evanescent events
sombre situations
soothing and seething
a sea of tedious troubles
a stream of turbulent tears;
As pensive memories
overflow the frontiers
of this stupefied heart
the tides of tomorrows
erode the outer edge
of the uneven circumference
of this unfulfilled life;
the dark shadows wait
prowling like wolves
like suicide squads

make inroads into peace;
At the edge of the horizon
a ray of hope shines;
as it dubiously twinkles
the voyage of life ends.

A Pair of Sparrows

The rays from the east were not so cruel
the bamboo cot was pleased to bear my frame
under the cool shade of the guava tree
The touch of my love's hand was soft
gentler than the caressing breeze
On the green and shady bough
two twittering sparrows steeped in love
vied with each in showering its essence
their beaks became one at its peak;
our eyes met in lucid glow
her clasp grew firm though soft
with her ear close to my heart's beat,
her eyes drew an unearthly graph.
Their unintelligible notes
steeped in the balmy nectar of love
touched our hearts – a tender touch
that tuned the strings of my heart
and sent vibrations of serene joy
that found loving communion
in the mute song of my love
with whom I shared the bliss of life
in joy or rest or sleep or strife.

University Wits

Poor I uneasily went and went
round the so-called learned and stout
like a satellite around a planet
till my shoes wore out
for the so-called guidance;
They always seemed to be busy and ideal
but indulged in gossip idle;
Killing the radiant self-respect
on the altar of dubious quest
to gratify the ego of the eccentrics

that delight in practicing tricks
I stepped like a devoted cat
into the sanctum-sanctorum –
their hallowed cubicles
with hollow brains and bicycles;
The room was as cold as a corpse
full of volumes, bound and buried;
His eyes winked through the spectacles
but feigned to go through lines –
live electric wires to such lives;
At last his languid lips lisped
and the Delphic oracle came :
'I am too busy, I can't spare
five minutes till two summers'.
Summers rolled like somersault
winters wailed like Epsomsalt;
Bowing my head and selling my soul
bending my spirit and mending my sole
I climbed the steep cliffs,
and offered my hair to the Lord of the Hills;
The subterranean voice echoed the place
"May his soul rest in Peace".

A Seminar

One sunny September
atop the snowy Himalayas
assembled a few stately crows
from states far and near
to discuss their mite in music
feats and flights in the airy realm;
some played merrily and sang freely
while other dark dons from many angles
displayed their peevish plumage
stood by the capital native stock
said in an irate grating voice
'We alone can sing and fly.
how can others sing or vie?
We will scissor their feathers
and roast them if they try',
Their loud notes and tall talk
buried the melody of the rest
Till then they could not rest,

beneath the pines in their nest;
The umpire's gentle cry turned sour,
Terrorism swayed and danced –
Sivathandava of the white crows
on the snowy flakes of Dhawaldhara.

An Interview

One sunny afternoon
I entered the universal gas chamber
suffocating with brows high and low
Voices cracking, croaking and crowing
Where hours burnt like camphor
on the Royal altar of Alma Mater
emitting pungent fumes of sulphur.
The room was deep and wide
as coy and quizzical as a bride
a relic of medieval glory
transplanted with the Hilly grace;
Yonder on the revolving throne sat
the grand sire to select his progeny
on the pseudo lines of epiphany
with the satellite of expert knights
imported from distant planets
to give succour to homely kites
and exhibit chivalry with their bayonets;
Aladdin's wondrous lamp was dim
before the cabal's magic wand
that delivered many a doctor slim
for whose healing touch craved the band.
While angels gazed with pensive looks
arch angels dozed on tawdry books,
the earnest groaned under the weed
till their lucid hearts burst to bleed;
the campus flowed with the stream of his breed
who could propagate the cream of his creed;
As gales of regalia kissed his frame
the sons of Shadwell reigned supreme
wielding the sceptre of caste and sloth
and shielding their brains from glory's path;
Creative work was never a credit
while the garrulous tongue the only merit,
Show and shallowness filled the grace

while true values fled in disgrace;
as a rule the wise were overthrown
while the wiseacre adorned the throne;
On crows and cranes the mantle fell
while the swans flew from the hell
with a sighing smile to snowy hills
to sing their songs with the flowing rills.

That Thing Money

Without that thing money
you are nothing in this sphere,
it alone has the alchemic power here
to change the baser metal into gold;
with its infernal magic touch
the gross becomes great
the low the high, the foul the fair;
In the current scenario
flow of currency is the vote bank
it makes or mars the crown;
It is not how you get it
that matters in this world,
It is how much you have it
that matters most;
The end winks at the means
and sinks all the diverse creeds
If Adam lost his divine Eden
Mammon restores the earthly Paradise
and mocks at the Saviour with his lures;
It is the oil that moves Fortune's wheels
and the wheels of Phoebus's chariot;
It changes an ape to a demi-god
and reverses at the zenith of pride;
Even a corpse needs coins
to enter a quiet dusty grave
and escape the steely puncturing beaks.

A Bubble

Who is to whom in this world?
All the familial bonds
familiar ties and chains
dilute and disappear;

I entered the stage alone
and nude without a shred of thread
and so shall I leave it
at the inevitable hour;
In this interim period
in the fog we croak like frogs,
we are swayed by the tides
of love and hate, warmth and sloth
and drowned by tidal waves of lust;
While we thrive, friends throng,
they cease to come near
the moment we cease to hatch;
Spouse spurns and child chides
As you quit this coloured cage
you are sent nude and alone
assigned to flames or dust;
What do we have here,
what do we carry from here?
With all motion and emotion spent
life is a bubble, a bauble;
who's to whom in this world?

The Bicycle

Saviour of the poor and the low
the pupil, the peddler and the page
you light the twinkling candle aglow
in the faint eyes that lose the gaze.
And lend your chaste heroic wheels
to the wearied penniless feet
that feel sore at the plodding heels
averse to move in hostile heat.
With ways inscrutable and canny
you race through ways wide and tiny
glide through field or jungle path
tedious or devious without fear or sloth.
Alike the rich and the rag you treat
enthrone them on the sagging seat
and their train on your neck and back
while your slender sphere shrugs on the rack.
Propped by the wheeled wings of a fairy
you carry sacks and loads sundry
and appear in many a form and guise

a mobile house or loaded cart at sun-rise.
To an alien mind or a Western eye
the sight of your racing frame yonder
with tiers of toys, tins and boxes high
placed on and around is a unique wonder.
You too have your pricks and cyclic seasons
you arrive like a bright cherubic bride
grow to a matron proud of her sons
and decay deformed after decades of ride.

The Coconut Tree

With its legion knotted roots
firmly planted in the sandy soil
like an angler's fishing net
the coconut tree stands like a giant
that stoutly defies the Olympic Powers;
With its fibre-firm and fatty base
its tall trunk is rooted to the post,
like an undaunted sentinel on guard
it defies the force of wind and flood,
till it breathes with its matted roots
it fights and falls like a lone hero
when it is cruelly felled or uprooted;
Human hands never intend to torture it
aching bodies crave to lie in its shade
Its fanning leaves, a lush-green canopy,
kiss the lucid starry sky, cheer the sphere
and bless the weary animate world
with cool shade and balmy breeze;
It throbs the poet and thrills the lover
it gives succour to the sick and the thirsty
while its kernel pleases the cook and the palate;
While the dry leaves help the poor man's hut
its coir adorns the royal chamber,
Without its aid and selfless help
neither the temple bells ring
nor the wedding bells nor the knell;
It lights the eye and delights the heart,
Its breathing body is a work of art
that creates concentric circles of joy
and unfading halo of aesthetic delight.

The Cloud

Yonder the churlish cloud at the east
flies fast as if for the feigned feast
with his impish vapoury brethren
with his dark wings on eerie weather
at the sight of the starved and parched
or flees on the flood of foaming fleece
rich with pearls of piercing showers
that rips and peels its airy skin
but fill with resurrecting manna
the pining buds of fragrant flowers;
it shakes the sepulchral firmament
and the vast terrestrial sphere
with its aerial thunderous roar
and blinding cosmic brilliance
and soothes the world with its magic arch;
It deludes the humble peasant
whose eyes are glued to the stars for survival
and whines at the parched furrowed field
and frightens the famished cattle,
has no sympathy or pith of pity
for the rows of vessels near the tap
that clink, clank and clash
at the hungry roasting meridian hour;
It moves like a grey chameleon
incarnating many a livid and living role
an elephant, a lion, a serpent
a lying leader, a beheaded hero or a ghost
or the map of a country or a continent;
Amid the sea of apathy it is our friend
a friendly messenger of the airy realm
sailing over hills to distant shores
conveying tender thoughts of weal and owe
to the members of melancholy heart;
With the capricious clouded grace it rains
and dispels the clouds of ills and pains;
on earth it is the surging spring of life,
on it depends existence or extinction of life.

The River

I am as old as the lofty ageless nature

She is my only friend of noble stature
Service to mankind is my only duty
Which for ages enshrines divine beauty.

I hop down from the top of the hill
And rush through bush and briar with skill
Pit and pond to the brim I fill
Water on my bosom is sweet and still.

I chatter and ramble through pebbles
Producing melodic rhythm of bubbles
I swiftly tumble into turning tracks
Rumble and leap into rocky cracks.

Through many a zigzag path I hurry
Many a nameless plant and rock I bury
with valour I leap into the valley
And soon I make a sudden sally.

Streams and brooks are my relatives
To our Lord, the Ocean, we race like fugitives
With our pace and race in glacial symmetry
Passing through many a town and cemetery.

On my huge breast lie many a bewitching ait
Which to the beholders gives a charming sight
A sandy bed under the crescent moon-light
Well nigh fishes hop in the fulgent night.

When enraged many a village I swallow
Submerging fields pregnant or fallow
When people grow vile and vicious
Through floods I teach a lesson specious.

I pass through idyllic pasture grounds
And slide though groundnut grounds
Indeed, my buoyant joy knows no bound
When I gaze at the flowery plants around.

Joyous lovers wander on my sandy banks
Rest on grassy beds men of all ranks
Poets muse on my lap in solitary hours

I fill their minds with creative powers.

I linger under the moon and milky way
With argent-tinged foam and froth on my bay
Singing amorous songs with boundless pleasure
Having the mild windy wings as my treasure.

Science has grown and grown and grown
I have to groan and groan and groan
My full freedom has been curtailed
By tying my legs with dams wide and wild.

The Rainbow

The mystic rainbow dawns in the sky
the sober soothing sign of pallid calm
after the densely dreaded dance of storm,
the thrilling celestial arch so nigh and high;
Its quiet cosmic genesis is loudly foretold
by clouded thunder and lightning bold,
The enchanting colours of the aerial pride
vie with the bright bangles of the bride.
The gorgeous garland of haunting hues
shining with prismatic virtues of dews
kisses the peaks of the two hemispheres
of the ethereal bride free from fears;
The wondrous bow of Indra ringing rapture
legion hearts and souls on earth does capture.

The Supreme Lord

I am
the burning flame
that springs from fire,
the fleecy wave
that dances on the flood,
the linear ray
that traverses from the sun,
the luminous halo
that girdles the moon,
the rapturous rainbow
that bedecks the sky
and enchants the world,

the glittering silvery line
that laces the gloomy cloud,
the thunder and lightning
that bless and blast the world;
I am the here and the now
the there and the then
the ever and the never
the what, the why and the how
the when and the everywhere;
Those that believe me
bathe in the Manasa lake
and reach the celestial land
spread with gold dust;
the rest know no peace or rest
and end up in the dust.

Pensive Memories
(Chennai, Poets Press India, 2005)

The New Year

The year departs leaving in its gloomy trail
many a bleak memory of unfulfilled desires,
pensive paths of dark days that often wail
and haunting moments of chasing cold fears;
The New Year with uncertain hopes sets to sail
to reach the solid shores of success bright,
gives us renewed vigour and zeal not to fail
amid the weird turbulent waves of gory fright.
May it brighten the days with melodic lyres,
banish the ghost of darkness from the sight,
sweeten the stream with fast vanishing pyres
and fill the wakeful eyes with a flood of light;
Cast thy winter weeds of cold woes and mopes
and put on the new garments of renewed hopes.

Can I Sing?

Can I sing
a sweet balmy song
with the rope tightening
around my groaning neck;
Can I dance
a dainty rapturous one
with bleeding feet
on pins and thorns
on the bleeding ground;
Can I smile
a sunny silvern smile
with a burning heart
when waves of flames
rise high in my bosom;
Can I think
a quiet sober thought

when this mind
the anchor of thoughts
has become dull and dry
dry as dust and bones;
Can I see
a clear inward perception
with these myopic eyes
blighted and unlighted
by back-biting and jealousy;
Can I die
a quiet and easeful death
with a mind full of cares
and body full of sores and snares.

The Bridal Bosom

The far off clouds in the azure sky
touch the tender strings of my heart
with the magic wand of amorous showers
Million fresh and fragrant flowers
with greeting petals bloom in my heart
The pretty pearls behind my budding lips
yearn to smile with the laughing jasmines
Incessant showers of tender thoughts
fill my bridal bosom with thrill
Let me race with the silvery rays
let me play with the caressing wind
in the milky light on the milky way
I wish to sail with the gentle leaf
In bouncing joy on the lucid lake
and fly with the icy fleecy flake
Free from care I wish to leap and hop
and float on the flowing foamy crest
and rise as a ray in the dawning east.

Bride's Wishes

Her heart floats on fleecy clouds
her bosom sails on ethereal wings
her merry meandering thoughts
lift her lithe frame to cosmic heights
where awaits the nectarous nuptial bed
bespread with fair fragrant flowers;

heaving dreamily on joyous jasmines
her body flies beyond her rational reach
and thrills at the Bohemian beach
the sweet embrace of her fancied man
her unknown adoring destined hero
lingers long with transporting kisses;
The sweet music of her bridal bangles
wafts her on the breezy waves of bliss
where her serene soul sings to the rainbow
which she wishes to bend in ecstasy
to see the unseen spheres of joy;
The milky shafts of the silvery moon
gently pierce into her dreaming heart
and kindle tender flames of lucid love
with caressing breeze in her bridal bosom.

An Orphan Lad

With his soiled sooty clothes
dishevelled hair unkempt
and unwashed underfed body
he sweeps the compartment
carpeted by groundnut chaff
with his ragged and ruined shirt
His eyes glitter at the coined charity
his teeth shine at the shining coins
The pitiful sight of the orphan
to vultures is a matter of fun
Him the proud and the prude shun
He lies on the friendly pavement
and sleeps on the filial platform
on a freezing Christmas night
like an unclaimed disowned article
floating on the slimy waters of Lethe.

Migrating Birds

Silent shadows with sunken eyes
walk along the dusty country road
with bags of ragged clothes and utensils
on their drooping heads and shoulders
with their famished cows and calves
whose ribs project from their hide

in search of distant green pastures
and fields that need working hands
while their women meekly follow them
in soiled saris with deep dull eyes
with their lean and skinny children
that are hardly strong to smile or cry
with a faint flicker of horizontal hope
in their listless lustreless passive eyes;
Others have gone to other lands in trains
some with tickets and some without,
For miles and miles the hostile heat greets
the raucous rays of the wrathful sun
and the hot windy music from rocky ravines;
They reflect on the old men and women
too old and weak to move from their huts
that stay with heavy hearts near empty hearths
and hunger-hollow eyes exhausted with tears
Migrating birds look back in a pensive way
on wings weak and weary that can't fly far away.

Without You

You are
the melody of the music
the balmy breath of the song
the beauty of the flower
the glow of the smile
the solace of the rain
the charm of the rainbow
the coolness of the moonlight
the sweetness of honey
the purity of milk
strength in every step
the healing touch of the herb
the warmth of the world
the life of the light
the light of my life
Now, without you
all is dull, dry and dross
life still devoid of thrill
with neither flavour nor savour
loses its soul and sense
this part of the heart cleft in twain

craves to meet the other, the better one,
in the other world far away
with the aid of the baffling death
a welcome friend and guide.

Unpredictable Man

Humanity surges and sails
People flood and thud everywhere –
schools, stations and theatres
shops, slums, lanes and streets;
Sky is wild with rending cries,
the earth teeming with legions;
We have only sounds and sounds,
sounds discordant and grating
like the croaking of frogs,
braying of asses, barking of dogs
jaded jackals and filching foxes;
Where it moves, why it moves,
when it acts and what it does
even their confounded creator
cannot explain or foretell
nor can he conjecture;
The world has fast outgrown
his infinite vision and ability
None can predict or define
the odd unpredictable man
at once a man and a monster.

Maya

All the world is a huge illusion
This life an alluring snare, a *Maya*;
Birth and death two sides of tinsel coin,
No mirth in birth on this dusty earth
No dread nor fear nor pity in death
Multiple phases and varying hues of life
Are like chameleon's changing colours,
A leather bag hiding bony flesh and blood
A gall bladder full of air and bile,
A tiny puny puppet on the fleeting stage
Gaping and aping others in the play
Run by the great Genius high above;

All this love, lust, hate, ire and anger
Carnal quest, thirst and hunger
Lose their pith and layered mazy meaning
In this meaningless hazy hurried journey;
In this colossal weird world of stunning *Maya*
Frame and shame, sun and shade
Joy and sorrow lose their odd identity
And merge in vast colourless vacuum
All pomp and pride of earthly *Maya* fade into dust
The divine Maya mocks at the signatures on water.

The Power of Love

It is an end, but not the end
it can bend the body but not the spirit
and drive people mad, rich and strong
but it is timid before those who defy
and welcome with a thousand hands;
it flees and flies from shifting sands
till it flees and flies from shifting sands
till it gets its dreadful chance
and picks the naked bones in ruins;
Until its hands are strengthened
by battering blasts of stormy winds
it can't pluck a petal of a flower,
but when it falls to windy blows of rain
death mocks at the petals dead as nails;
Lovers may die but not their love;
death may have its sway on all,
but it bows before the Lord of love.

Assembly of Quadrupeds

A vegetarian tiger addressed the assembly
of all the quadrupeds in the capital jungle:
Thanks for reposing rational faith in me
and voting me to power for full five summers,
With wolf as my Premier, progress marches
Socialism sails and democracy dances
We assure you free supply of food and shelter
gas and grass, cheese, ghee and geese,
liberate you from the yoke of taxation;
Like the biped leaders let us not graze

stealthy grass and fatten with corrupt crores,
Let us strive unreservedly for a merited society
free from caste or class, creed or breed division
where cows and my tribe, wolves and sheep coexist
in a New Atlantis with a new millennium vision.
All the members present felt freshly elated
roared and lowed, barked, brayed and bleated
in a singular note of democratic approval,
while crows, cranes and eagles joyously flew
above the fabled feline head a dozen times
blessing the enthroned leader free from crimes.

The Lotus Palace

The Lotus Palace stands
a solitary brick and mortar tower,
gazing down at the millennium dust
that engraved the paled ages of mortal glory –
a dumb witness to the decay of prided lust
a lone sentinel guarding down the hill loyal
the heart-sizzling ruins of rulers royal
a glory, a wonder and once an envied Paradise
razed by savage hands blind and unwise;
Surveying the skies with a sneer, the storeys
relapse into past woven with storied histories
while the ground, a mother without relief
bereaved and broken, lay still in grief;
Royal rooms studded with spider's web
in nocturnal internet with bats racking rub;
The chiselled gods and goddesses scattered lay
mute and mutilated at an unholy havoc's bay;
Lotus with lovely petals shines and smiles
with eternal faith at the passing clouds
changing shades and marching miles.

A Pair of Doves

A pair of lovely doves atop my house
cooed and kissed amorously all the day,
The female lay eggs and both guarded them
one relieving the other to go for food,
Both alternately fed their young ones
by filling grains into their tiny beaks;

The little ones clung to them and grew in days,
It was a happy home, a mini Paradise;
The female fell ill and rested in the nest
The male flew restless around the nest,
sat beside her, kissed and consoled;
The day dawned, the spouse woke up not,
The male cooed and touched her with his beak;
It was removed, but he stood there
waiting to see his spouse with listless eyes;
Young ones flew; still he waited there
lone and lean without the spark in his eyes;
With Eve's exit, Adam lost his Paradise.

The Ganges Flows

The Ganges flows deep and dreary
muddy and murky, miry and weary
at the divine feet of her Lord Viswanath at Kashi,
confounded and dumbfounded by narrow lanes
alleys and unnumbered snaky bye-lanes
surrounded by snake-plaited fake Swamis
famished Sadhus and fattened cattle
heaps of garbage and rising dung-hills;
He shut His two eyes at the foul play
rampant in His house and uneven vicinity,
His Third eye terribly quiet with the Trinity;
When it opens is beyond the human ken
When it does, it is beyond the poetic pen.
At Gangotri, the serene seat of sylvan scene
In the lushy lap of the snowy Himalayas
celestial Ganga sings with a silvery smile
and in rapture dances like a sprightly girl
hopping from hallowed heights with crystal purity;
As she leaps to the round at Rishikesh
she bangs at the door of the busy populace
who cruelly pollute her virgin innocence;
As she travels fast reflecting hard and long
she bemoans her impure state all along
and shares her sorrow with her two sisters
at Prayag-one visible and the other unseen,
having hid herself shy under the ground
from the doom of polluting human touch;
Paying heed to the call of Kala Bhairav of Kasi,

with self-restraint she reaches Varanasi
like a pregnant woman to meet her Lord
no longer able to bear the long separation;
content with her union, cherished long and blessed,
with her living Lord, the Lord of the Universe
she purifies mind and body with her alchemic touch,
even bones, ashes and corpses, left in her waters;
Vedic scripts and epics spring from her waters
As Ganga flows the culture glows with life divine.

Do Thy Duty

'Do thy duty'
said the wise Lord ages ago
on the battle plains of Kurukshetra –
the right remedy for the cancerous evil
in this land of sloth and acts uncivil;
Ours is a land great and glorious
of many saints, seers and Rishis pious,
a land of great culture and heritage
many a learned school and hermitage.
The God came in many avatars
as the land badly needed guiding stars
and His drastic help to check the tide;
Standing on the battle plains wide,
He preached morals and morals.
As such we are ready to preach and teach
and play nude at noon on the golden beach;
We are averse to put it in practice;
While all others enjoy, why shouldn't we?
Others are there to do, not we
We look at them with malice;
The Lord gave the Sermon on the Mount
Sermons flow like perennial fount
from the tipsy lips of our lusty leaders
who crawl, climb and kick the ladders,
with their bulging purses and stomachs
full and fat to the bursting point;
with joy and dark victory they anoint
their headless heirs with heartless heads
to reign the soil from their sullied beds.

To My Other Half

This moment is a lifeless moment
an unbearable and an accursed one
that marks the arrest of the Universe,
the final futility of the fleeting life
of all living creatures from the hoary dawn,
that life is ephemeral and momentary
a fleeting bubble, a flimsy bauble;
a moment when half of my breath
is arrested unawares and sadly lost
when my better half breathed her last.

Ah love, my paralysed pulse still vibrates
though for ever yours ceased to pulsate;
Why this ghastly gesture of animation
when it has lost is seminal meaning,
Endless is this airy eerie night
No light in my life nor use of light
when the light of my heart is put out;
For whom should I resume in vain
this life's lame lonesome jaded journey
Why this rough rudderless voyage?

Your exit for me is a sudden deluge
a mortal blow to our conjugal bliss
that left a smarting dent in my spirit
an atomic explosion in my happy heart
leaving an endless saga of sheer sorrow
The flames of your pyre on the river bank
have engulfed all the five elements
rose high and burnt the sooty skies
leaving a burning pyre in my mind
and rising flames of sorrow in my heart.

This heart overflows with gushing grief
mind is flooded with your tossing thoughts
that race through eight and twenty winters
All the waters of the seven seas
are transformed into salty tears
that melt and spring and flow
in rising tides from my harrowed heart

there is not my spouse my beloved mate
to check my inner sorrow's spate
no way nor solace to this desolate fate.

Mother nature with flowing memories
of your playful vivacious early days
generous deeds and innocent ways
bemoaned your sudden untimely end
clouds roared and poured torrential grief
streams and rivers overflowed with tears
The clouded sun covered his face in sorrow
the moon and stars hid themselves
screened by clouded drops of downy rain
The sky burnt with the pyre of meteors.

O moon, don't look at me in pity
Peep not at earth deprived of my love
Her two eyes are two lunar spheres
Whose light is marred by cruel Fate
that plays a gory game with puny mortals
and leaves me in endless darkness
Legion luminous lunar luminaries
can never equal the light of my life
The light of my eyes and house is put out
Changing my life into a cursed night.

O love, your lively loving presence
Lent my average life rich fragrance
Filled it with sweet essence of flowers
gave fairer fruits I never dreamt of
created million melodies in life's voyage
churned sweetest drops of honey
tuned the lyrical strings of my heart
and solaced my tired sentient soul
with your radiant smile and balmy touch
Why have you vanished from my life?

Like a dream, like a wave you came
entwined my life like a lush creeper
lifted my soul to dizzy heights of rapture
warmly opened the doors of Elysium
and filled my life with heavenly joys

But what have you left me now?
Ashes of your pyre that consume my heart
Tender haunting melodic memories
Why have you done like this
Why have you left me alone in tears?

O dear! Your mind was clean and clear
word, thought and deed pure indeed
face fair and gentle and heart tender
The result of this sudden end of yours –
Your release from all worldly bonds and fears
leaving my sorrowed soul amid a sea of tears
A fatal blow to our conjugal love and role
a deadly arrow that rent our single soul
A pair of doves together fly in vernal joy
while I am doomed to sail alone as a toy.

Ah love, to whom shall I talk and confide
To whom can I open my heart's inside
With whom can I share joys and woes
How shall I bear this onerous burden
You left unawares on my heaving head
without your smiling surging solace
How can I pull this life's heavy cart
When my head breaks with your parting
This is my destiny's crazy whimsical song
My half-dissolved life's melting melody.

Then this life was a sunny stream of poetic joy
with sylvan scenes and sublime symphonies
Sans you it is a desert, a vast dark abyss
The past a smiling spring of pastoral love
Present a curse of meaningless vacuum
Tomorrow a stifling shadow, a horrible dream
The rest, full of unrest, a painful reminder
a deserted temple without the goddess
My joy and solace lie in living in the past
In the balmy embrace of the sweet memories.

I felt gracious God made us for each other
Though my half, you became my whole self
To me this truth is beauty and divinity

Why is it belied by unkind baleful fate
O Lord, why have you punished me so
O Shiva, are you justified in doing so
Ah love, without you in this shallow sphere
Why should I breathe and move alone here
You are my God's gift and my breath
Without you why this journey on the earth?

I have not the strength of Saadhvi Savithri
to convince Yama and fetch you alive
But I wish to reach you and pray the Lord
that after fulfilling the task you left
the moment my pining breath stops
my searching soul should unite with yours
before His Lotus Feet in the world unseen
from where no one has ever returned
Ours is the sacred *Saptapadi* bond eternal
that unified our hearts with spirit supernal.

Sabari

It was joyous spring with lushy breezy green
Dandakaranya was rich with many a sylvan scene
The Chitrakuta, an awe-inspiring mountain
surprised with many a rill and chill fountain
Down the hill it was punctuated with trees tall
Peepal, banyan, neem, tamarind, teak and sal
while boughs of *neredu, regu, velaga* and *panasa* bowed
with fruits of varied shape and taste much loved
It was abound with creepers full of leaves and flowers
which bloomed with lusty touch of tender showers
Malle and *nagamalle* whispered to the caressing bees
that sucked the juicy sweetness to the tasty less
Yonder the Pampa lake shone in glittering gold
as the bright rays of the sun kissed the waters cold
its bank, like a gorgeous girdle of solid gold
studded with precious stones in a fairer mould
had a bridal look, daintily dressed with flowers
of hibiscus, *mogili, sampangi, ganneru* and *ponna*
that attracted bees with dainty drops of manna
a wide range of shapes and rich rainbow colours
All these filled the place with a fragrance sweet

and sights delightful – for the eyes a feasting feat
The sights of the swimming fish banished all the woes
gliding swans lifted the soul to the skies from throes
the two Princes Ram and Lakshman, pure and peerless
radiant with divine light, bold and fearless,
with their locks of hair knotted on their heads
their necks doubly shining with rosaries of beads,
with bows in their hands and quivers of arrows
behind their shoulders that paralysed foes in rows,
paced forward sucking Nature's amazing beauty
that dispelled their gloom and kindled their duty
Well nigh on the bank of the tranquil lake they saw
The Ashram, the seat of beauty and serenity, in awe
There deers and monkeys played on Nature's stage
Sparrows chirped and doves cooed in dainty love
while pretty parrots lisped on many a leafy bough
At its entrance with folded hands there stood
sacred Sabari, a woman ascetic, old, feeble and good
welcomed the princely brothers with all her heart and soul
'O Ram, my life is blessed at your sight sacred
your visit to my humble hut has blessed my life's role
My service to Guru Mathang, the sage sacred
did at last bear unparalleled fruit celestial and sweet
by realizing my life's dream of worshipping your feet;
The great sage long ago with his celestial sight
saw your coming in a halo of heavenly light
He advised me ere his march to heights of heaven
with a heart full of kindness for this poor servant
to wait and have your darshan with hope fervent
and make my life divine to reach the dreamt of heaven.
Kindly accept my humble hospitality to-night
please taste these fresh forest fruits ripe and rare
whose quality I tested by biting each in earnest right
Only to see you I postponed my death to this hour with
care'.
The royal brothers in joy accepted her hospitality
their tired bodies rested and blessed her with nobility
The old woman disturbed them not till they awoke.
The next morning, after ablutions, Rama spoke:
'Sabari, you are a pious, noble and sacred soul
Kabandha extolled you and Rishi Mathang's role
would you show us the mysteries of his awesome Ashram'.

Ignoring her aching senility that needed Vishram
she in joy showed them all the spiritual glories
and spots of the seer's abode that could stun the fairies.
Knowing the cause of their sorrow and mission, she said;
'O Ram, dispel all dark despair from your noble head
Seek the help of righteous Sugriva in the nearby hill
Success is yours and to your ideal and virtuous will'.
In grateful joy Sri Ram, God-incarnate, spoke
'Your kindness drove our fatigue away as we awoke
Mother, you appeased our appetite with delicious fruits
choicest in these woods and tasty nutritious roots
May all your penances guide you to heavenly poise
You are free to choose a sphere celestial of your choice'.
The aged Sabari, dazed in joy and supernal ecstasy
wasted not a moment, lit the pyre as in a fantasy
and leapt into it chanting Rama's name filial
as her divine form ascended to the world celestial.
The noble brothers, divine avatars on this earth
blessed her soul and went in search of Sita of divine birth.

Tsunami

A sudden traumatic shock, a terrifying wreck,
to the soaring space scientist a quaking check,
an unprecedented Nature's callous calamity
leaving horrendous death toll, a grim reality;
In the ghastly guise of a *Tsunami monstrous
Deadly death rose from dark depths unknown;
Sea exploding in fuming fury fully blown,
the earth quaking and crumbling losing all patience
ravaged the coasts, isles and whole nations
from the far off Sumatra the epicentre in Indonesia
to India wrecking the Andamans, Nicobar and Malaysia;
Whole families and villages drowned and wiped out
hundreds of fishing hamlets swept away in a bout,
thousands marooned and thousands snatched away,
Thai's thrilling Phuket and Phi Phi isles washed away,
Once an enchanting scene, now a yawning grave;
Coral isles and idyllic beaches from Sri Lanka
to Thailand, Malay and Male reeling in carnage
The grand Galle Stadium in wreck and dismal visage
Marina Beach, a place of sunny sandy bloom
In everyman's reach wears a deserted look of gloom

Reduced to a soul-sizzling scene of tidal doom;
People of all ages, men, women and children
Before they knew what happened or tried to run
Were caught unawares, crushed and washed away
by the massive palmy waves in full frenzied sway
leaving a horrid haunting vacuum to grin and greet,
catastrophic havoc callous, cruel and complete;
Are they beaches or bleeding open air mortuaries
sylvan seaside scenes or corpses-filled foul sanctuaries?
Hundreds and thousands in mass graves laid,
covered with bulldozed sodden earth their only aid,
Can hundreds of rescue ships, planes and trains
revive the lost melody in the benumbed brains
of the bereaved souls, battered, bruised and beaten?
Can devastation be so sudden, so cruel, so cryptic,
so abrupt, so terrifying and acidly apocalyptic?
Indeed as ants to human feet or flies to wanton boys
so we to Nature's fury leaving a trail of hushed noise.

*A terrible tidal wave, a colossal natural calamity, that occurred on
26th Dec 2004 in South East Asia that devoured more than a lakh of
people and left a higher number homeless.

Gliding Ripples

(Baltimore, Pub. America, 2008)

Erase the Borders

Cool down my friendly foe,
the beaten track let us not toe,
let frenzied fears and tears fly,
free from missiles keep the sky;
Forget thy fierce frozen frown,
let fanatic fires cool down,
erase the burning borders,
freeze the towering terrors;
Boundaries exist only in mind
whipped up by theories blind;
Let us not race for winning runs,
in one voice wipe out killing guns;
emotions rise high in cricket mall
but let not a pawn or a wicket fall.

What is there for Pride?

Man, stop thy thundering pride
and its roaring plundering ride,
it is a fast fleeting fading tide
that vanishes after a glowing glide;
Go to any land or liberal State,
feel its pulse and pregnant fate,
What is there for human pride?
except a crazy galloping ride;
Fly and race with a noble role
from east to west or pole to pole,
see any history, turn its pages
till this day from bygone ages;
What is there for human pride?
Pages red with pitiless helpless blood
darkened with its streaming flood,
vicious lust for power and wealth

to grab the crown with sword or stealth;
in joy they sell their swollen soul
to reach their guilty golden goal;
to clear the way they kill their kin
without a thought of heinous sin;
they build their vast bleeding empire
on innocent blood and burning pyre;
When time calls and gives a sign,
tyrants fall, and fades their reign;
When Fate summons depart we must,
All this parading power goes to dust.

Mortuary of Books

As I move slowly down the aisles
and look at the racks full of heaps
I feel haunted by the pensive looks
of long-buried and forgotten books,
the treasured souls of sages and ages
of varied wings of global knowledge,
trimmed, bound and buried here;
its heavy breath heavier than dust,
layers of decades of choking dust
on their sighing virgin breasts,
piled on defaced decaying coffins
hiding the light of the departed souls
suffocates our breath and brain.

Books vomit words without a pause,
now their solemn stony silence,
intriguing to its depth, awe-inspiring,
does not augur well for the state;
They are cast away, the untouchables
innocent offspring, poor victims
of their aged thoughtless creators,
destined to reap the original sin
of mimetic creative arts and science,
fallen under the guiding curse
of vanishing stars and inspired hearts;
Books fail to seduce eunuchs,
sigh and lie undisturbed in Yogic sleep
like innocent babes still in cradles.

Is it a mortuary of blighted books
guarded by moths, white ants and spiders
or a place for lice, flies and butterflies
to roam, gossip and exchange looks
or a domed Taj to spell academic doom?
Some day their angry hungry spirits
in utter despair may rise and revolt
with fallen and stolen pages as sabres
to kill and purge the lazy brains
of ignorant wits and feigning scholars;
Let the long forgotten fallen angels
wake up from torpor and resurrect,
break the fetters and regain Paradise;
May their creative spirits in fury rise
or the setting sun may never rise.

A Broken Life

He sits on the broken bench blankly
at the tea shop at the busy centre,
holds his cup of tea so firmly
as if he would not get another,
with his beard unshaven for days;
lovers of tea come and go from all the ways
without a break from dawn to dusk
sipping tea amid all political husk;
workers without work culture
employees without a sense of time
from nearby offices come with customers
burn a cigar with tea for an hour or two
in this favourite Kerala tea shop;
Still there is tea in his magic cup,
drinking tea is an art to sip drop by drop
without a drop entering the thirsty throat;
six to eight in the evening he sits and sips
looking into vacuum at passers-by;
I too forget or fail to count his sips
to count the sips is to count the drops;
I try in vain to catch that feeling
beneath and beyond his blank look;
His eyes lost the real sight a decade ago

when his only son was killed in War
in War at the burning N-W border,
the body did not come, shadow returns;
All these cups and drops fail to trace
the missing son, the missing joy,
and draw his broken heart's ECG;
The graph of the curling fumes of tea
fail to draw his life's ship wreck,
while the mirror on the wall mocks
at the broken pieces of his bruised life.

Idols for the Idle

As a little boy at the village school
my mind absorbed from my teacher
visions of legendary idols –
        Sri Rama, Harischandra, Hanuman,
        Krishna, Buddha, Christ and Kabir
who steal our hearts for ever
and inspire eternal values.
At high school stage,
stage is set for history page –
        Asoka, Akbar, Sivaji,
        Napoleon and Lincoln.
Soon the blazing flame of freedom fight
and sacrifice seized our minds straight,
new visions of idols marched –
        Vivekananda, Aurobindo,
        Tilak, Gokhale, Gandhi,
        Subhash Bose and Patel,
who shine still and linger long
and kindle the spirit of National Song.
Alas! Old idols lost their light and lustre;
later I grew up to this Nuclear age
which has led to the primitive stage
with dilution and pollution of culture,
radical revolutions to rob and grab,
education to extinction and execution of ethics;
Crazy idle brains worship false Gods
and install in the sanctum matinee idols;
Underworld dons don the robes of role models,

hypocrites, gangsters, scamsters and criminals
are now in line for the covetous claim.
　　Can we see the fading ideal vision,
not the trumpeted vision Twenty-twenty
of market values breaking the backbone,
but the vision of lasting human values,
the noble vision of shining moral values.
In queue our cruel competitors stand
to seek the princely bride's jewelled hand;
Whom Fortune favours Time will decide,
but Fortune is as blind as Justice;
Let us wait and watch till Doomsday,
till then, may God save our country!

A Forgotten Bird

This village has a name
which has erased my image
from the green foliage
of its unnumbered pages
growing from its distant roots;
A decadent decade ago,
in a dusty shaded street
in a vernal nest on a bough
there nestled a pair of doves
with love, love as the only breath;
The female hatched eggs with care,
the male flew and fetched grain
in sun and shower and fed them,
she flew with the young one with ease
over hills and rills, vales and woods;
one morn her wings failed to move,
her loving heart struggled to beat,
the male saw her mate's exit
with a helpless heart in grief; .
the living bird flew depressed
in search of peaceful pastures.
A few colourless summers later
he returns to his native nest
to relive his treasured memories;
fellow birds ignore him as a stranger,
village wears a commercial look –
the same sunset and rustle of leaves,

but the night stretches endless,
in intoxication lingers long,
darkness dances in the graveyard;
The forgotten bird with tearful wings
flies aloft from the forgotten village
with pangs of pensive memories
and coldly haunting apparitions
to distant hills and horizons.

Let us be Human

As children play with dolls
decorate them with flowers
making merry cries and calls
under shady boughs and bowers,
men of all climes and ages
of varying parts and stages
play with man-made toys
designed to their whim and choice;
fancied images or idols of Gods
become sacred symbols and Lords;
As fiction becomes a rooted fact
fancy loses its proud impact,
blind faith springs instead,
severs the reasoning thread,
kills the coolly thinking head ;
Frenzied men wage power wars
which they proudly call Holy wars,
though heads float in blood
that flows like a furious flood!
Let us strive to be human
and drive the spirit inhuman.

This Restless Race

Why all this mad restless rattling race,
mindless gasping and wild pursuit,
no calm or joy in all the livelong days,
our basic spirit this greed does not suit;
He surely knows limited are his days,
hoards his wealth in banks and biscuits;
still he craves to earn in devious ways,

and hides the excess beneath in iron caskets.
After all, this earthly life is a fading bubble,
why weep or gloat over what is not yours,
why all this fret and fume for the rubble;
We are tiny toys to play for Higher Powers;
When this breath ceases, depart we must
to embrace eternal rest in the earthy dust.

The Rose

My presence is a source of pure joy
even for a lifeless idol or wooden toy,
To all I spread full fragrant light,
even flinty hearts I fill with delight;
How I dance in springing breeze!
Even wasps and buzzing bees I tease,
Quietly I sing to the tunes of spring,
to the old and young equal joy I bring;
I preside over all the festive days
from birth to death in royal ways;
I get my place of pride in any land
in worship or wedding as rose garland;
I am the peerless queen of flowers,
blushing brides adore my rose showers.

It faints and falls helpless on the ground,
pale and lifeless without demur or sound,
deprived of fair and fragrant floral wings;
it is removed with all other unclean things.
Next morn comes the dull untidy maid
to clean the fluffy floor though unpaid;
All the petals, withered and trampled still,
found their cemetery atop the dunghill.

Donkey

His highness the dauntless donkey,
rid of all the back-breaking load,
feels as bold and free as a monkey;
struts on the dusty rustic road
of the near deserted toiling hamlet
thrown on the bank of a dry rivulet,

distracted by stray barking dogs
lustily leaping over stones and logs.
Monarch of the sole solitary street
kicks the ground with unfettered feet,
proclaims proudly his loud royal state
revolting on his fabled frazzled fate
with a loud brazen bragging bray
that echoes the vale with acoustic spray.
He wishes his master to bow and kneel
and dreams to conquer the unkind humans,
who always beat his tribe, whip and peel,
with his regal mercy steeped in patience.

Mosquito

Monarch of eerie clammy night,
an unkind despot blood-thirsty,
fond of pond and puddle dark and filthy,
a nagging source of uneasy fright
to all on the earth that happily breathe,
old or young with or without teeth.

Its unrivalled savage stinging reign
extends to all the land, water and air
by all means fearful, foul and unfair;
expands soon with scanty seasonal rain
over huts and palaces with cryptic ease
defying all en route like a devil to tease.

On invisible wings singing it soars
well nigh the zones of stink and stench,
stagnant tank, pool or oozing trench;
sucking blood in mad triumph it roars
and builds with ease its fortified empire
to keep its progeny far from fear or fire.

We sit and stand, feebly frown and fret,
we lie, roll and pull our legs in sweat,
hands scratch and itch, clap and clasp,
but it steers, veers and flies from our grasp;
it outwits, beats and bites us from top to toe,
and revels in humming joy our royal foe.

We spread with pride the mighty net
to defend our smarting skin helpless
from your daunting storming threat
of infectious malarial invasion ruthless,
from you and thy impish ilk and kin
who stand by you through thick and thin.

Toddy Tapper*

He keeps himself hale and hardy
with meat, mate and mug of toddy,
extracted every morn in earthen pots,
brought from the village potter in lots,
hung on the sliced tender blossom
atop the palm trees on airy bosom.

He climbs the prickly tall palm tree,
free from fear and tension free
swiftly with his subtle wonted skill,
to others a wondrous feat of thrill;
the twisted rope around his waist
like a blushing bride's golden girdle
does all the climber's guarded miracle
ensuring his balance safe and straight.

Half naked at every dewy dawn
in sweat or shiver every morn
he stands at the foot of the tree,
at a wink he is at the top in a spree
to tap and collect fresh toddy;
in the art of tapping he is never tardy.

*Mildly intoxicating fresh liquor extracted from blossoming fronds of
palm trees by skilled workers, known as toddy tappers.

Watching the Sea

The infinite blue expanse above is clear,
the deep blue sky is wild without fear;
the silvery moon rises cool and clear,
the milky way is bright with cheer
with ravishing twinkling stars
radiating their rays beyond Mars;

I stand on the soft sheet of sandy shore
gazing at the vast blue expanse before;
As I watch the roaring militant waves
kicking the solid shore, hills and caves,
waves of thoughts tease and toss my mind,
a complex maze difficult to unwind;
This terrestrial sphere seems to melt,
all things bubbles and baubles fade as felt;
time past and present, tied to future,
merge into the timeless without rupture,
lose their disfigured shady identity
and move ahead as a single entity;
All this march of ego and human pride
with its hissing echo is a futile ride;
dissolve all its meaningless strides
in the ebb and flow of tossing tides,
leaving a haunting echo of oceanic music
merging in the eternal note of cosmic music,
the divine spread of harmony universal
balancing the irreconcilables colossal.

Selfish World

Who is to whom in this world
It is a gruesome greedy guild;
If the need sharp and selfish ceases
flowing and flowering love freezes,
you are thrown out as an addled egg;
if they need thy help, they kiss thy leg,
embrace you with a scheming heart
full of guiles, wiles and wily art;
if not, doors close with a bang
and echo with a hostile hissing fang;
Alone you may wither or shiver
in scorching sun or pouring shower;
all thy kith and kin wisely forget
when shining coins you fail to beget;
if by chance you fall on evil days
they shun you as a leper without grace;
all the near and dear shun your sight
till you loathe your shadow in fright;
There is nothing truly to claim yours,
there is none whom you can call yours;

In the end what remains is muted dust
whence we come and to dust go we must.

Body and Soul

They alone are wise
who know and see the self,
They who know the self
grieve not at death or decay;
it is the body that dies,
not the shining spark of soul;
even after the exit of the body
exists the deathless soul;
This body of flesh and blood
is a fading bubble ephemeral,
self is real, soul is eternal;
Soul leaves a body after its death
and enters another, fresh and new,
just as we discard worn out dress
and wear another new and fresh;
This body is the tabernacle of the soul,
Grief and passion belong to the body
and confine to the physical brain;
they cannot touch the soul,
they spring from fleshy bonds
far from the transcendental plane.

A Mother's Cry

'Won't you give my beloved son back,
with folded hands I beg and prostrate
to put our life's wheel back on right track,
we worship you; don't seal his fate.

Why do you tear and burn my womb
and hide my only son in your hungry womb?
Swallow me but spare my son and send him back',
mourned his mother till her heart did crack.

The old mother beat her chest and cried,
cried and cried till her eyes sorely dried,
all her cries failed to reach the roaring ear;
consoled her his friends who returned in fear.

Two days ago her son sailed in a boat
to fill his basket rich with catch of fish
with his friends singing a lyrical note;
storm lashed in fury and wrecked his wish.

A high whirling wave struck his boat
in full fury, the broken boat did float;
Unheeding the dark cloud and weather report
he braved the rising wave near the port.

His nets danced with the reeling tide,
Fish he caught breathed free and safe to ride;
he ceased to struggle with the mighty wave
which tossed his breathless body brave.

Ignoring that morning warning call
sailed the fisherman young, bold and tall;
while his friends returned on wind's vicious turn,
he sailed on whirling waters never to return.

She stood on the shore from sunset to sunrise
and wept with flood of tears in her eyes;
She wept and wept till no tears were left,
though her heaving heart was in twain cleft.

Her blank eyes stared at the blue expanse,
for days and days she stood with no response
till that fateful eve when the roaring wave
took her to meet her son in the watery grave.

Pair of Eyes

A pair of eyes at the corner Ice cream parlour,
for one so pretty there is no need of beauty parlour
which often as a rule ruins natural beauty
which fairer sex visit as part of their office duty;
eyes? no; two moving magnets of living art
with power to pull and enthral a flinty heart;
quality ice cream cone in her tender hand–
how can you fix or quote for this ice any price
as long as it is there in that magic wand?
Mobile phone in the other with her touch

alive with her breath whispers music rich;
her icy eyes chase with the speed of flavoured spice
and leave the throbbing hearts full of heaving sighs;
taste of ice cream goes to airy heights divine
once it gets the touch of her lip's gentle line;
lips? No; they are ravishing petals of rose,
her sailing sari end, a dancing flower as it knows;
It seems a fairy descending is gliding in the air,
luminous lamps pale beside her face of beauty rare;
eyes refuse to move from her toes that tune on heels
as long as there is an enchanted heart that feels;
it is stupid to look at child's cone ice cream
when there is brighter beauty's embodied dream;
half blooming from her budding lips her smile
dances still after a weary travel thousand mile,
and tunes my heart's strings in melody sailing soft
as ripples rise in calm waters as breeze wafts aloft.

My Roots

With passion
and rare compassion
you rightly understand me
to the bone, to the marrow bone,
to the bed rock, the bottom stone,
to the core, to the inner pore.
If I look at the green leaf
even for a while very brief
or at a jasmine in full bloom
or in the corner the blinking broom,
even if I touch, an evanescent touch,
too brief, really not so much,
but a beaming particle of rice
only once, not twice or thrice,
or the embers that make waters hot
and kindle my inner heart,
I feel the fragrance of thy breath
stronger than the aroma of rosy wreath;
All things that you touch,
even the dust with thy casual touch,
fill me with films of ringing love
to relish the nectar like a dove,
taste and bask near thy isles and peaks

and see the roses fly to thy cheeks
and suck the rosy blushes to the lees;
You can never desert me
even in dream or desert, my oasis;
By any ill luck if you leave me
and this world leaving me to grope,
thy memories are my prop and hope;
I wish to cut my ruined roots here
and find them in thy loving sphere.

The Other Bank

On the other bank
of life's racing river
winds blow in a whirling spree
sing the dirge in wild tune,
Waters flow in swirling flood
swallowing lives and livestock,
suddenly recede and disappear
leaving one long winding stretch
of sand and slime, weed and reed;
hope with bruised feet
plays the lame beggar
evasive and evanescent,
stands on its last limping legs
and sings the swan song
in empty spaces on the flute
looking with vacant eyes
at the distant grey skies;
Silence in frenzy yawns,
roars in fury and yearns
to devour the remainder
by transmitting the signals –
the signals of wild silence
primitive language of emergency
echoing the lonely landscape
transformed into a ghostscape
and engraving on sand the epitaph
of the final terrestrial epitaph.

Be Calm, My Dear

Be calm, my dear,

don't weep, drop not a tear,
I can't see these tears
dropping down your eyes,
I know you can't tell lies;
Tell me the thing
that torments you
and weighs you down;
Unload your heart,
by disclosing without art
it becomes light as air,
mind as soft as a feather;
your luxuriant hair
flies without reins,
it requires combing
as does your heart;
Waves always don't rise,
they pause as your cries;
See! The sun rise
has a new look
sending rays of hope,
your eyes get a new light
to set matters right;
Let thy painful memories
fade, fade and vanish
like autumnal leaves
giving way with a ring
to a new smiling spring.

The Bridge

For many limping years
till the award of grey hair,
whole without a black,
I have travelled
across this slighted bridge
a span of only a few yards
linking two opposite roads,
otherwise isolated identities
always opposing ways and views
never willing to compromise;
The bridge, broken-hearted,
crashed and was swept away
in the hostile current;

It is built afresh to act
as a peace maker with tact
somehow to reconcile
the irreconcilable ways
by cementing a compromise –
a united path to be wise –
of sand on sand with sand to stand
till the issue of cheque to withstand.

Our Leader

A lone man to lead he stood,
en route all hurdles he withstood
like a big banyan in storm
or a captain with vision in form;
Crowds as flocks did follow
his fat white-clad shadow,
thicker than his gory riches,
taller than his free promises;
It wisely bulldozed their fates,
Moths fell at the lighted gates.

Peace and Love

Latest product in the global market –
'Peace & Love: Two in One': a craze to stop wars,
made on the Moon, tested and tasted on Mars,
available now in malls and Super marts;
Buy now or never, Stop & Shop, live and love,
in piecemeal or wholemeal in containers –
whole food, both organic and inorganic,
well designed and organized well to sell
in attractive bottles like McDonald's,
lowest price, no expiry date, valid till you expire,
updated with hi-tech formulas and equations,
fresh arrivals in sealed cups and capsules too;
incredible 'Never before' publicity in multi-Media,
a blaze on TV, rage in Newspapers and wall posters,
echoes on pulpits and platforms, piers and pyres,
near nude nymphs, our lovely torch-bearers
flying on supersonic wings from East to West
spreading the burning flame of peace

in all the five elements in atomic pieces;
See & Buy, Buy &Try – a rising star, a rage;
Buy one, get one or get lost with a bonus tea,
Peace and Love, Two in One, rolled in one –
Peace in love or love in peace in eternal bliss
or peace and love in pieces in Metro Malls.

West Haven Beach

It is a cool evening, gently warm
in early summer with traffic jam;
dark woods stoutly kiss the coast,
tall inspiring trees are our rustling bards,
strong singing sentinels our coast guards;
cool breeze gently wafts as a sailing kite
warmly willing to kiss but hesitates to bite;
lush green carpet stretches along the beach
a place to kindle love divine and preach;
a soft sylvan bed greets pairs of doting lovers
and cools with sudden summer showers;
The young, old and gay, dance on the beach
to the melodic tunes of guitar within the reach;
Adults spend lazing on the soft sandy shoreline
while kids play and build nests that shine;
Summer concert on the beach fills the sky
with old dancing hearts ready to step and fly;
At the farthest end of the endless expanse blue
rises the orb of moon in robes of milk white hue,
the light that gives strength to guide
the groping man to cross the adverse tide;
East and West may not meet and merge
but white and black, red and brown
live as one without a faint hint of frown,
a single stream moves with a human urge.
Note: West Haven Beach is in Connecticut State, U.S.A.

Living Word

Sitting on the green grassy ground,
decked by flowers and plants around,
guarded by majestic maples and pines
by the highway with glittering lines,
with the quiet Atlantic waters nearby,

patches of fleecy clouds scanning the sky
after a brief spell of summer showers
bringing life to fading flowers and bowers –
celestial messengers who calmly vow
the aerial visit of the wondrous rainbow
that fills all hearts with ethereal joy,
a splendour of magical colours to enjoy,
I reflect – a quiet spot serene even in storm
throbs the heart with Nature's beauteous balm;
The frontage of a huge Church mansion,
for man's faith in the Lord a solid version,
proclaiming His gracious Living Word,
a glowing message from Lord's ministry
free from unclean political chemistry,
a Living Word to create a living world,
to fill it with His grace and love
free from stain, pure as a milky dove,
An ideal place to inspire new prophets
Christ or Krishna, Buddha or Mohammed
to come and spread the light of Living Word,
the gospel of peace and love to this groping world:
In this garden of Eden, blessed thrice,
let us not open Pandora's box and be wise
to resolve the paradox and re-create Paradise.

Note: Lines written in honour of Living Word Academy, Church
Ministry, a spacious campus in West Haven, Connecticut, U.S.A.

Sherwood Park

Is this the bewitching seaside beach
kissing the scenic sylvan Sherwood Isle
that launches one thousand cars free from guile,
ten times the number people old and young
spread on lawns and stretch of sand;
by one and all the scenic beauty is sung,
tired souls get relief from kissing balmy breeze,
silent waves whisper mild magical tunes
rustling leaves sing merry welcome tunes;
blankets and red carpets spread on green carpet,
tents with festoons of coloured balloons attract,
wooden benches alive with beaming festive faces,

hot packs and packets of wholesome food;
culinary fires beneath the cool canopied trees,
bread and beef, chicken and bacon rolls,
warmly fry on burning sparks of coals;
ovens, metro and micro, greet hungry eyes
with delicious smells of barbecue and spice;
Feasting brunch and lunch on the sandy beach,
cake, bread, butter, jam and sauce entice,
salad and juice follows an egg sandwich;
dance and music on one side, games on the other,
walking and cycling in delight go together;
Some lie on the sand and relish sun-bath,
a few stand and gaze and others relish sea bath;
While boats sail to the island shore nearby
thousand gulls glide on the sea and fly;
Some wine and dine in warm sunshine,
others sit, sip and gossip with hearts frank,
lines of colour or creed find no place or plank;
A touch of gipsy life to the cream of culture,
charming beach by the waters of the Atlantic
fills the hearts with warm thrills of the romantic.

Note: Sherwood Park on the Atlantic shore in the South of Connecticut
on the way to New York is a favourite picnic spot in Summer.

Oh, America!

Oh America, thou art a miracle,
fabulous land, thy word is an oracle,
thou art a single star in high advance
faster than fair and fairy France;
Woman's high heels on the far off moon,
the sun of life style at the vertical noon;,
Roads and lanes look spick and span,
unclean and uncivil ways people ban;
No piece of paper or butt or pup's litter,
unending lines of racing cars glitter;
Sky high towers and huge shopping malls
fill our eyes with thrills of Niagara Falls;
Men and women always run and run,
work and work and never shirk for fun;
The more you work, the more you earn,
the more you earn, the more you burn;

No way, you are forced to spend
No chance to save or your fence to mend;
By any stroke of fate if you fall ill,
coffers of medical doctors you fill;
they loot and suck you to the last drop
till like an autumnal leaf you drop;
Hi-Tech robbers in medical mall
cashing on health, the wealth of all;
Sundays are busier than other days,
fleets of cars at beaches and on highways;
Stay healthy, stay in America in joy
Work and work, earn and live to enjoy;
If yourself, by any lapse, you fail to insure
Your life's boat is sure to sink, be sure;
If you fall critically ill and on evil days
'Fly to India' wise man of the East says;
Surgical or spiritual care costs very least,
The sun sets in the west only to rise in the east.

Niagara Falls*

A marvellous sight in this terrestrial sphere,
Niagara! Rich in charm thou art Nature's wonder,
Almighty's chosen spot inspiring awe and fear,
Beauty of the Bridal Veil Falls none can plunder;
Gushing waters leap with a wild splendour,
Mighty minds and heroic hearts for ever explore
the racing waters falling with ceaseless thunder,
the terrible beat of the Horse Shoe's hungry roar;
The magic spell of the Maid of mist's white robe,
Nature's gifted child, symbol of frenzied freedom,
binds people of all parts and faiths of the globe,
Enchanting fury! a divine dot in God's kingdom;
The massive cataract makes all human pride bow,
Heavens bless the Falls with rare magic rainbow.

*Niagara Falls is a massive cataract on the river Niagara that divides US
and Canada. The name was given by the land's first inhabitants, the
Neutral Indians; the word Niagara means 'thundering waters'. Close to
the American Falls there is the smaller one, the Bridal Veil Falls; the
Canadian Falls are known as the Horse Shoe Falls. The popular tourist

attraction at the Niagara Falls is the *Maid of the Mist* boat cruise which
carries passengers into the whirlpools beneath the Falls.

Mahabalipuram*

Breathing blocks of monolithic shrines
along the sparsely verdant seaside hills
arrest the wheels of Time with sculpture lines;
their chiselled charm with thrills all the ages fills.
The sand and stone, endless sea and shore
sing the aesthetic glory and pomp of the Pallavas,
and echo the sculptured beauty on billows' roar,
that glows for ever through the chariots of Pandavas.
The mute melodies of the chiselled classic art
fill the sky and the hoary land with rich heritage,
tune the symphonic strings of enthralled heart
and transport the mind in trance to a bygone age;
Sculptors and their patrons faded into dusty page
leaving their deathless art for eternal gaze.

Note:
* Mahabalipuram, one of the UNESCO's World Heritage Sites in South
India, was a flourishing sea port during the days of Periplus (1st century
A.D.) and Ptolemy (140 A.D.). The major attractions of Mahabalipuram
are 14 rock-cut cave temples called *mandapas,* 9 monolithic shrines called
rathas and the famous Shore Temple. These structures were built by three
successive Pallava Kings – 1. King MahaendraVarma (600 – 630 A.D.), 2.
NarasimhaVarma (630 – 668 A.D.) and 3. NarasimhaVarma II (680 –
720A.D.) who developed the Dravidian style of Temple architecture within
a short period of a 100 years.

My Humble Prayer

Listen to my humble prayer
if you have ears, Oh the Supreme Lord!
the Almighty Creator of this awesome Universe,
boundless and baffling, mazy and amazing,
in thought and deed an incredible wonder!
Bless me, a poor soul, if you have grace
in thy unseen all-embracing cosmic heart,
to see the priceless treasure of mother's love,
to suck the ecstasy of love of the loving wife,
to enjoy the blissful joy of the child's smile,
to feel the rhythm of the rustling leaves,

of the caressing breeze and the singing bird,
to drink the beauty of the cheesy soothing moon,
the twinkling stars afar on the milky way,
to rinse the rhythm of the flowing waters
hopping from rocky hills and snowy peaks,
the ceaseless music of the roaring waves
on the endless stretch of blue expanse,
the soft caressing touch of the fleecy cloud,
the falling drops of rain, celestial messengers
that bridge the aerial sky and the earth,
to swallow the deafening sound of thunder
and suck to the lees the thrill of the rainbow,
feel the terrible silence of the deserted graves
and taste the bliss of thy divine radiant grace;
I pray to Thee, the unseen One, Oh my Lord,
listen to the humble prayer of the simple bard.

Echoes
(N. Delhi, Gnosis, 2012)

Human Touch

You have travelled a long way,
into the lonesome land of darkness
leaving a trail of haunting blindness;
At the start you were a little human
now you have strayed far far away,
confounded at the fatal crossroads
sadly weighed down with woes,
pricks and tricks in heavy loads;
in fact the exact root none knows.
The route is untamed and unmapped
while thy moves and moods overlap;
alien control of your blood and bone
forbids you to see the shades of tone;
Your name is now grossly forgotten,
your return route is totally rotten,
the journey is fraught with risk
your steps can no longer be brisk,
can't keep the track of footsteps
through night's unintelligible silence
that can't be deciphered by eye lens
until you reach the Utopia of Eden
and breathe the breeze of the garden,
that alone can give a fresh lease of life
to arrest the play where crime is rife
and impart a piece of human touch
for the groping man a faint crutch;
substance and shadow in right mix
can deliver the man from the fatal fix.

An Echo

We think we are unconquerable
but we are still so miserable;

How long do we see the rehearsal
of this dull replay of the shadow
of the bereaved truth, a widow?
Light, its might, with its clean burial
in unclean infectious environment
haunts in dark rainbow colours.
The rocking doubt and denial
with shocking incomprehension
hurls us into the desert of contradiction
that transforms itself in its flight
into an enveloping veil, a wail
in the fog of veil, a vicious wall
of thick despair, the arrested air,
breaking dreams into pieces,
a mirror dashed to the ground.
The long awaited storm leaves
in its trail the calm, the callous calm,
the uneasy calm of the burial ground,
yields a wide wild range
a concrete change, a challenge;
overnight a line of light streams
through the screams of hunger,
the veil, the cloud, dissolves;
reed, a weed, transforms to flute
leaves a halo of sweet echo.

Untraced into Dust

As beauty with truth disintegrates
in mausoleum fancy hibernates;
Slowly moving in this historic town
that is made and unmade every day
I reflect upon this desolate royal palace*
built heroically a thousand years ago
that stands now in ruthless ruins;
the sight squeezes the heavy heart
with the horrible wreck of art,
a moving image of concrete fall
the ruined circuitous fort wall,
temples razed to the ground,
the broken rock-cut entrance
guarded by the sculptured Hanuman**
a mute spectator of the havoc inhuman,

the strategic curves to strike the foe
Do you hear the ominous sound?
The hooting of the owl spells doom
with the reacting deafening bark
piercing the eerie desolate land
deserted king's palace tower,
a relic of sculptured splendour
an aggrieved soul of bloody wars,
monstrous greed and callous neglect.
The gory hands and fanatic heads
that wrought havoc with blind hatred
left the stage untraced into dust.

*Refers to the King's Palace, built in 1000 A.D. at Chandragiri, near
Tirupati, Andhra Pradesh, India and to the Fort which was the last
Capital of the once glorious Vijayanagar Empire in South India after the
destruction of the famous capital Vijayanagar as a result of the defeat of
the King by the combined Muslim forces in 1565 AD. In 17th century
the fort and part of the palace and temples were destroyed by Muslim
rulers again. It is now one of the Heritage Sites.

**Hanuman was the great devotee of Sri Ram the hero of the ancient
Indian epic *The Ramayan*; Vijayanagar Kings had the figure of
Hanuman in their flag.

Nature's Play

My heart opens like a lotus
blossoms like child's smile
to see, hear, relish and feel
Nature's countless miracles,
gentle zephyr of cosmic music
soft, inaudible and eternal,
the invading flood of fragrance
of jasmines, lilies and roses,
lush leaves' gentle rustle,
sylvan wood's soft whisper,
koel's song and wind's stir,
animal's helpless whimper,
the terrible roaring beauty
of the vast deep blue expanse,
the soothing melody of rain
linking earth and sky like a chain,

the thrilling celestial rainbow
with her enchanting colours,
the awesome jewelled beauty
of the boundless starry sky.
I can feel the clock's beat
amid the scorching summer heat,
and the politician's stamping feet,
the foul smell of officer's seat
and orphan lad's piercing wails
that traverse on parallel rails;
I hear the resounding sound
of the tyrant's pounding feet,
the thunder and the stormy wind,
eternal music of oceanic waves
and Nature's art of Luray Caves*,
the thundering roar of Niagara
the icy touch of the Himalayas.
Nature's play of balancing
is superb, a wonder, a marvel,
a mystery we can never unravel.

*U.S. Natural Landmark, most popular, largest cavern in Eastern
America; located in the Shenandoah Valley of Virginia, 90 minutes drive
from Washington D.C.

So Tall and So Small

How this sudden change
incredible, so terrible a wide range!
Yesterday you looked so strong and tall
and strong as a tested concrete wall;
could a few rounds of the clock
give an irrecoverable lasting shock
to a man as defiant and hard as a rock?
too proud and headstrong as a lusty bull
with bellowing power brimming to the full
when decades failed to have any impact
on the stream of his thoughts minus tact;
Nothing remains in the land of remembrance
hardly an event suitable to an eye lens,
but a single day, a potent fateful day
could command the entire life with its say;
All banks of wealth he got with his muscle,

multi-million projects he snatched with muzzle
couldn't rescue his only heir from jaws of fate –
the sudden air crash, piecemeal tragic state;
Suddenly you, so tall, look so sullenly little
All your bragging bones become so brittle,
Your eyes with blurred skeins of memories
blasted by the invading blows and worries
get wrapped and trapped amid jarring voices
the ordained result of thy cumulative vices.

I Need a Base

I need a solid base
To stand and see, glean and gain
the strength to tell the truth to the race.
I need an environment
free from pollution, clean and clear
to live and breathe without fear.
I need work culture
free from the tribe of vultures
that feed on corrupt bread and bribe.
I need a will strong and firm
to steer through stormy tide
to the shore as a surer guide.
I need a friend to rely
in pain or gain or any weather
and in storm who would never belie.

Life on Wheels

I have scuttled and shuttled too long
between workplace and native place
for over decades of drudging years
amid oscillating tides of fret and fears;
Commuting the hot distance to and fro
between two hostile points, dead ends,
uncompromising with unbending bends,
life full of dents has become decayed,
to learn better things unwisely I delayed.
The unending and unfeeling black rail track
hurls me heaving with a load on my back;
loudly mock the irreconcilable lines
at my irreparable life with pallid signs;

this life on wheels finds peace at neither end
fails to deliver rest or any warmth lend;
how long this life on wheels moves
or when it derails or falls, who knows?
Maimed memories coolly sail in a row
and touch as biting flakes of snow;
on the other side of the commuted days,
consumed aloud in unnumbered ways,
yellow leaves greet with stony silence
to the autumnal bed beyond the tense..

Organized Violence

Often I hear with haunting fear
the volcanic sparks of silence
emitted by ceaseless violence
across the burning borders
exploded by imported AK47s
and inhuman human bombs,
tender teens trained by Satans
rolling in dark devilish masks.
The inaudible eddying current
generated by cloudless torrent
engulfed by clouds of fumes
of exploding powder of sulphur
has filled the land full of gloom
with redoubled vigour to bloom.
The disorganized vacant slots
create panic in fortified spots;
All these peevish pulpy seeds
coexist against odds with weeds;
breathing hemlock they grow up
in their prime to be blown up.

Search for Peace

Let us search for a safer place
that gives a slice of peace
in this dark confounded land
without the aid of a magic wand
through confusing landscapes
terrorist attacks and seascapes
and unearth the buried wonders

of the neglected ruined capital*
of the long forgotten empire.
Here sovereign tense is strangled
between presence and absence,
present neglect and past havoc,
in this no man's desolate land
deprived by the warmth of the sun,
encircled in the snaky coils of smoke
emitted from the bowels of the earth
hiding the burnt and razed palaces
haunted by unseen swords and spirits.
Let this historic search with firm root
deliver soon an enlightening fruit
in the dim light of the midnight sun;
the whirligig of time is smart and sharp
to silence the killer and the killed
in a wild weird play for ever chilled
amid the exploding volcanic trend
and lead to the dark destined end.

*The ancient Royal Palace at Chandragiri, built in 1000A.D. See the
footnote for the poem no.3. Refers to the history book *A Forgotten
Empire* written by the British historian Robert Sewell.

The March of Time

The clouded mind struggles
in this hurricane-blasted ship
in its voyage for a ray of light;
The spirit, tossed in the sea
of shifting incomprehension,
has lost the right direction
the true nucleus of existence;
Branches that liberally spread
generous shade are cruelly cut,
eerie emptiness looms and yawns
as I see with impaired sight;
premature pluck of the fruit
has axed the tree to the root.
As helpless children we witness
this magic of life in wilderness
spread on the terrible landscape
of life and death with no escape,

the puzzling play of entry and exit
from the noisy stage partly lit;
sounds of cocks and cockerels
fill the stage for proud laurels
and are soon silenced at the peak –
the magic moment mute and meek.
Can't we steer to a safer shore
from where we can soar and roar?
Let us counter with a flowery wreath
the encounter with unfulfilled death;
This aged blood can't arrest the moment,
nor can it reverse the march of time
nor can it activate the failing rhyme;
How long can we travel with sore feet
on this aimless pathless unmapped land
holding a blade of grass as magic wand!

Don't Fear, My Dear

Be bold, my love, I'm with you
unlike the days when I was away
for months, a few years even,-
the nature of the work was such
we couldn't help – for a paltry pay,
the only means of our sole sustenance,
often on other works enjoying myself
visiting hitherto unseen places and spots,
and those painful days away from you
I spent in vain at the looting capital,
fleeced and cheated by money squeezers
and licensed office robbers, bandicoots
when I couldn't follow your signature
that showed as clearly as an x-ray
your hypertensive blood vessels
the signs of which stayed undetected
in the early days of our wedded life
that moved on lines of the rainbow
of innocence and rapture and then
on neighbour's battlements and suits
your heart never did sink or shrink,
and in fact your words were my prop;
but from this Diwali you are weak and timid,
hostile to your grit, wit and character,

though the doctor says it is only viral fever;
don't fear, my dear, I'm here with you forever;
I can't bear to see a tear in your eye,
for children's sake muster courage
and soon this fever and fret will go,
we will celebrate our wedding day.

Rhythm of the Rails

I have boarded the train
which I never wished to;
the one I wished to left
before I could reach it;
now I am forced to travel
without any reservation
without any motivation
to stand and await my chance
amid the noisy riotous mob
with commuters, wage workers,
students proud of copying
in the examination for a grade,
teachers indulging in that trade
and other travellers hurrying home.
We do not know what awaits,
let me not succumb to baits;
The desired track I couldn't catch;
the changed course let me watch;
In due course these lines may mould
the crossing lines of my life, my fate;
life is a compromise at any rate.
Now I travel alone by the last train
and attune myself to the rhythm
of the cold unfeeling iron rails
tantalizing to my vibrating brain
doubtful of reaching the destination.

The Inner Call

I have journeyed too far
through blind alleys and curves,
My silvery grey hair mocks at me,
I thought all the years green and gray
I was human among humans,

Now I see, how far from truth it is!
Neither am I, nor they *en masse;*
We all live in a world of make-believe
vainly trying to make others believe
while our smiles our intentions belie;
any move, it is only to the crossroads,
the inevitable wreck it forebodes,
terrible to think where this greed leads;
to what end all these rosaries of beads!
No way to save ourselves or our souls,
or our purblind priests and swamis old
when they are drowned in sex and gold.
We can't pin our hope on our leaders,
our cries don't reach their drunken ears,
as they sit on dizzy heights of booty
lie and roll, swallow and make merry;
At this late hour before the fated fall
let us not be deaf to the inner call;
ere the sun sets, let us sow purer seeds
and save ourselves by nobler deeds.

A Democracy

The land I walk groans under hostile feet,
biting grass, dry and cheerless, bites the sole,
hands grab my throat, I walk gasping blind,
claws snatch me unawares from behind;
I struggle to release me from the trap,
no way from this iron grip though I gasp;
whirling mind sees no escape route
from this vast treacherous landscape
which spreads like Thar desert on my shadow;
In the name of SEZ prime land is grabbed,
we poor peasants are by force trapped,
Ours is a democracy ruled by capitalists
where the booty share our pseudo-communists;
we are whipped to cast our votes to criminals
and stripped of our land and victuals;
on the voting day we have no choice,
suppressed is our chained voice
These leaders, in fact bandicoots, rule
on the ruins of our living skeletons
from the mazy mists of callous cities

encircled by burning barren landscapes;
their plunder marches with a thunder
from land to industries, roads to mines,
unhindered, kith and kin share the loot
like foul foxes at tiger's prey en route.
All around lies the stinking environment
looking with tearful eyes in torn raiment
at the exploding chaos and confusion;
Living by chance in fear and fright
humbly I pray the Lord to set it right.

Revolutionary Writers

With carbonated lungs he yells aloud
till it creates a ring of riotous cloud
on his pet topic of human rights
that puts out reason in dark lights
the cherished one that gives him food
and does as a rule no general good;
with the press he makes a hue and cry
at the death of a long wanted terrorist,
a record killer, a pseudo-communist,
with a huge award on his head;
his free lectures on class struggle
yield him rich dividends – a few sites
at the golden hills in the Capital
and a high rise elegant residence ;
his popular spicy folk songs
a raw rhythmic picture of wrongs
make him a man of the masses
who dance to his tunes as he passes;
when innocent persons and cops die
with bullet shots and in bomb blasts
champions of human rights seal their lips,
revolutionary writers show heels and hips;
our odd maverick leaders defend killers,
overnight they become political thrillers,
not a voice is heard denouncing the crime,
defence of human rights ends in rhyme;
till they see it in the press they can't sleep,
the starving media catch it in a leap;
their chaotic mind wrecks social peace
and cries aloud to get killers' release;

they relish to fight for the rights of those
who snuff out others' rights and lights.
All social ills ballots and bullets can't cure,
neither soporific songs nor ballads ensure,
change should come to make hearts pure.

Ashram

Saffron robe is his shining mask
to realize his cherished tainted task;
helpless religion falls an easy prey
to his sensual lips that feign to pray;
Brimming with desire his lustful eyes
greet fairer beauties, frail butterflies
allergic to austere ways and pressures
he seeks *mukti* in carnal pleasures
often at others' cost he goes abroad
to bask in pleasures full of fraud,
attends royal night clubs in jeans
and dances with tinsel fairies in teens
while fuming spirits lift him to heights
only to see his fall to abysmal depths;
he declares himself a living Bhagawan
and goes on a holiday in a caravan;
Lord Krishna suffers in his grinding jaws
while his ill-gotten wealth soars above laws;
Millionaires come and end in mystery
their burnt ashes arrest their history;
His ashram, a palace indeed, invites riches,
discards the poor and distributes ashes;
in the name of implicit faith in God
he makes gullible souls meekly nod;
His sweet nothings and charming lies
capture the rich and searching thighs;
he and his tribe to real sages are a blot,
but dark clouds can never eclipse the sun.

Life is a Tightrope Walk

This life is a tightrope walk
springing surprise and shock
a dangerous exercise for the livestock
one step forward or backward

leads straight to untoward results,
hurls us down to abysmal depth
downfall and ignominious death;
For some it seems an easy walk
a half step and jump, a long leap
to reach with the precision of a clock
their ambitious goal and turn a new leaf
by looting and uprooting our cultural wealth
through devious ways and acts of stealth,
loads his speeches with the spice of lies
while his acts are devoid of ethical ties;
his folk songs bewitch the masses,
his thunderous talk leads all classes;
wherever he walks his every step
creates an aura of false fragrance
unbearable with foul proud pep
springing shocks of new alignment,
his harangue gets a louder applause
from greedy parasites without a pause;
twinkling celebrities and glamour girls
that surround him and stay by his side
boost his painted image far and wide;
unawares in a moment a hair-split slip
hurls him down ending his high-rise trip.

Divorce in Verse

'We are a great nation
with dynamic vibration,
Our culture is big, great
and glorious at any rate;
Marriage is a mere contract,
a convenient mutual pact;
so simple, no more than that;
now we can't live together,
you Indians are uncivilized
and sentimental fools,
we can't observe rigid rules,
no dance, no spice in life,
Think, still I am your wife!
How long, I can't imagine!
Let us part and divorce.
To you is this word a shock,

your mind flat does it knock?
At least with divorce
life will not be worse;
you can soon forget
this fast and fussy wife.'
'Dear, life is a compromise
you know, you are sharp and wise,
think cool or we'll sink
Marriage is a sacred bond
It is not child's play'.
'Stop this childish talk
I thought in the evening walk,
Now no need to think,
this decision is final;
as friends let us divorce,
now search for a second wife.'
'Dear, you are my wife,
with all this still I love you;
at this rate as you say
I don't know in this life
who'd be my final wife,
the last one or the lost one.'

Sting of the Skin

Section: I

They rent out the skin
though yield is thin
hunger rebels
ignores ethics.
They are blind
blind to the touch
male and moral,
their need is such.
There is youth still
residue of beauty too
to meet their needs
their customers' needs.
Unable to bear the burden
they sweat, fret and suffer;
with all paint and perfumes
burning heart spews fumes.
With the sting on the skin

they are our disrobed nuns
or none even for fun to shun
our monks are above sin,
so are our sulky skunks.

Section II

Not willing to work
many seek easy money;
for them, it is not a fall
but a fall to rise, to be wise.
They know
they have crossed the line,
they know
customers are in line.
With masked status
they lie and live on lies,
they have money
to buy choice honey
neither pure nor clean;
everywhere adultery
an unbroken tradition.
Some feign to be pure –
unfulfilled urge
plays hide and seek –
seek pleasure to the pitch,
somehow to cure the itch
and graze in alien pastures;
For them the forbidden fruit
ripe with chemical heat
tastes sweet to the root.

Poets' Meet

Poets, pseudo and shadow, meet with quills
pruning their feathers to read and breed
atop Mt. Parnassus, the sacred Seven Hills,
to gain fame and spread their creed, a weed.
Many read their broken lines dry as dust,
idle men and media shower high praises;
others present their pale pages full of rust,
hollow heads and fans heap vanity prizes.
Our quills with poetic looks shine in state

sycophants heap eulogies on poetasters
who shine with caste and cash sans taste,
the latter flatter our flawed prose masters.
Some struggle to find a seeming image
while for others merit is a distant mirage.

Comfort Zone

Once when I was a college teacher
I heard of PM's visit to the town –
for an hour's stay in the guest house
toilet room transformed into AC room;
In those days we get up before sunrise
and go to the field to ease ourselves
with running water at arm's length
talking and pulling blades of grass
drawing diagrams on sand or dust.
Now things are different, facelift!
Remote rural house has a toilet
we decline to go to the rivulet;
in public places, trains and theatres
still they are foul forbidden zones
unless we arrest our dear breath
by practicing *pranayama* or yoga
or just postpone the urgent mission,
more often an unavoidable session.
I recollect those happy student days –
with problem in correct pronunciation
often lab. and lav. exchange their roles;
with sulphur gas and pungent smell
distinction is so thin even if you yell.
Call it with whatever name you like,
rest room or comfort or relief room;
In rest rooms in the US or the West
we feel relief and like taking rest;
here we feel like fleeing, too bitter,
in fact the sooner we quit the better.
If the room is clean and tolerable
for teens it is a private Paradise
where most of their budding skills rise.
We may not like it, but we can't resist
and in fact without that we can't exist.

The moment the release is over
spreads a wave of relief all over;
of the like we can't see or buy or try
in all the spheres known or unknown;
All unrest and uneasy tension vanish
and lead to peace with artistic finish.
After the exit of the unwanted stuff
emerge dynamic plans and decisions,
Spring begins with renewed visions.

Change!

Once from hungry stomachs cries burst
now from power hungry leaders' thirst;
common people remain helpless tools,
flow with the wind like yellow leaves,
they simply sit and see as willing fools
in search of a bunch of shining sheaves.
While hunger lies on the lap of sweat
our leaders in foreign trips rest and fret;
hungry wolves resort to wicked ways
to gain power and win in power race;
with idle men and women, hired lists
with spurious slogans, flags and fists
so-called backward and oppressed march
in fleets of AC cars with a burning torch.
Can such parades ever bring a revolution?
It comes through man's nobler evolution;
While our leaders indulge in foul ways
there is no hope of rise for our race;
progress remains an elusive mirage
till change comes in minds in any age.

Pillars

Speeches and screeches I hear,
as owl's hoots they pierce the ear,
from the greedy village heads
to the wily heads at the capital –
indeed a colourful capital show,
a dark downpour of words, a flow,
but not a tiny pure drop to drink
not a single grain to pick or think.

Swamis and Swamijis sit without bias
and message flows as milk from dais;
Their words like balloons go too high
and show the twinkling stars in the sky.
These leaders, political and spiritual,
fake and fraud, play roles effectual,
one in white and the other in saffron,
prowling wolves in lamb's skin,
shining to rob in borrowed robes so thin;
without fatigue the endless show they run,
to suit their ends words are wisely spun,
sail in the same boat to drown the flock
and climb the ladder on promises mock;
with ease minds of audience they throb,
helpless heads nod and doze as Roman mob;
One has mastered the skill to kill and chill,
the other the liberal art to fill and thrill;
the game repeat these pillars firm as rock,
our eyelids open only to close with shock.

Empowered Woman?

Even before sunrise she does rise
with aching limbs, yesterday's price;
in the morn her face shines afresh
as our Minister's white khadi cap
that glows as it rests on his lady's lap;
evening transforms her fatigued face
into a weak withered vegetable stalk.
She prepares her two naughty children,
sends the uniformed dolls to school;
half exhausted like a running machine
hurries to office with a harrowed mind.
With a borrowed smile on her face
she greets her friends at the work place,
and works with a mind without drive;
at five sharp she leaves the beehive,
hurries home in a crowded bus in a bid
to refresh her restless waiting kids
and her passive unconcerned husband;
late in the night the hard unfeeling cot
shelters the mass of her aching limbs;
Patience personified, she undergoes

this regular ordeal of servitude
yielding not a grain of gratitude.

Beauty Parlour

Though uncertain, after a certain stage
in this inexplicable quixotic stage
men and women with excess money
do try to buy or borrow fairer looks
drink delighting drops of beauty's honey
not with books but with cosmetic hooks.
Metro ladies crave for beauty with a craze,
to increase their looks run with a rage;
as a rule they visit the beauty parlour
a token of ladies' cultural valour.
Door opens and closes their pristine liberty;
on the revolving chair sits the high priestess
ready to perform the rituals of sacred duty
to propitiate the invisible beauty's goddess
by singing fragrant songs and psalms
and ready to scan devotees' palms.
The benign smile of the august lady
prepares visitor's twist of the body,
erases traces of care with her care
and teases her floating fragrant hair.
Like a lamb she sits in front of the altar,
faint music glides from the recorded guitar;
the poor victim at the operation table
spread with tins and vials with many a label,
pins, scissors, brushes, lotions and pastes,
paints, puffs and powders of varied tastes
guarded by a battery of transporting fumes
springing from scents, smells and perfumes.
Walls reveal mounted photographs
of mountain streams and naked nymphs.
Her sweet sighs and light screams
fail to arrest the volley of chemical creams;
heat and vapour her frail frame does relish,
her shining nails glow in French polish;
with stoic resignation she endures
the prick of the Himalayan herbal cures.
Tested skin spreads imported scents
that can infect the lighter minds of gents;

let our girls' faces be fair and fruitful
and minds clean with light fairly truthful;
beauty is as thin as skin, well we know
still we run after the vanishing glow.
Eve enters Paradise fresh and pure,
with forbidden taste she leaves unsure.

What is There to Tell?

Feel the silent sound
of the long awaited disaster
that leaves its incurable wound,
drink a glass of cool water
to cool your burning blood
that jets as volcanic flood.
In fact its hushed rocky tone
is harder than granite stone;
In this modern mall you can't find
all the things you need and want
though it boasts of A to Z of any kind.
Oh, here you search for grace
for grace there is no place;
you can pass through that way
say what you want to say;
be careful, there's the broken glass
a moment's carelessness
will make you bleed
and rot on the heap of weed.
About this life on earth
from the moment of birth
what is there to think or tell
a single stretch of greedy hell;
Again to play the game
on the transient mundane lines
is a matter of sheer shame.

The Silent Call

With the more designed dinner
which you would arrange
you won't cease to be a sinner,
your colour or role does not change;
the music concert full of rhyme

will not lessen your crime;
it may please the common folk
who are too small to share your coke,
knowing they are innocent
for your deeds can't you repent?
You did all the hellish deed
such was your state and need.
If you are quiet it's just a lull
we know you can never be dull;
the clout you enjoyed before
now you can't get any more;
your moves once bright as lamp
now miss the light, they are damp;
hear the roar of thunder
it does arrest thy act of plunder;
no less are your greedy plots
indelible are your burning blots,
your mindless material gain
hurled victims into a smarting pain.
In the avenging eye of the storm
we are fated to fail, though full in form;
the higher hand-shakes us to fall
and obey the echo of the silent call.

This System

You think
you can change
this system, this corrupt ink
it's not in your range
In fact you will change
with this infectious drive;
all your life you strive
see the yield, the progress
Super markets, I-MAX theatres,
Tech and medical schools
with super surgical tools
malls and MBAs that sell A to Z;
education is a commodity
a concept to sell in open hell,
Multimillion scams in stamps, dams,
in airy areas of communications
and in all the elements five

air, water, land, sky and fire
involving oil, gas, mines and power
aerodynamics and dynamites;
lives of gulls continue on shore
picking crumbs on the beach.
We never expect surprises
in these days of soaring prices,
only clouds of dust and gloom rise.
Today weather is west-bound
where plenty of wealth is found;
in fact the West looks to the East
as a guide for spiritual light
while the East rolls in gory greed
chanting the mantra of the past
and hugs the corrupt wealth at last;
without a sign of smiling welcome
seeing a sign of gain we come;
how long do we wait and grope
in search of an elusive ray of hope;
always we like to live on fields
they are our seeds and shields.

A Summer Trip

This summer, away let us run
from the pitiless hammering sun
and his smarting whipping lash
in search of a cool breezy wash
of the burning body and mind
in northern streams that run, wind
and hop from the mountain range.
Life in the South craves for a change
a day in April or May is a bitter pill
Fans run with the electric bill
without a note of warning bell.
Then let us go on a summer trip,
call it a pilgrimage or a holy dip
at Haridwar or Rishikesh, a tapovan
where divine peace ancient sages won;
the Ganges descends and moves on plains,
a dip refreshes and drives all strains,
crossing the river on Lakshman bridge
is a solace to the disturbed mind

and indeed a balm to the aching body.
The hills ring with the flowing music
of the rise and fall of the racing river,
echo the range of scenic splendour;
on the higher hills of biting cold;
Kerala tea is a high landmark,
Northern tea has the flavour of leaf
and the taste of the organic thief
hotels and taxis fleece your money
visitors' purse they suck like honey;
luring trade launches a long tirade
against ethics without any grenade.
At every tourist centre or holy place
commerce runs at a global pace;
from Liberty Statue to Niagara Hills
or from Rameswaram to Badrinath,
Tirupati to Varanashi or Kedarnath
exploitation is a common game,
things may vary, method is the same;
with time, line and length in mind
they smile and shine in cash and kind;
but in India the degree is of higher range
seeing which upright minds may derange.
In temples from south to north or Kashi
to a higher altitude like Uttarakashi
money buys Panda's impure blessings,
non-payment denies their looks and ashes.
Gods love to live and move on hill stations
and relish to rest on riverbeds and beaches
or on sylvan hills and cool mountains
with a high degree of aesthetic taste
far from the noisy crowd, a mass of waste;
but we are a race who never live in peace
and don't want to let them live in peace
we force them to share our common pains
and relieve us with a bribe of sinful gains;
with our desires tightly packed in a bag
we queue up and pray with a utility tag.
Spiritual quest is the common bond
that binds all the people of this land
from the seas to the northern snows;
it has the gravitational pull to attract

while in the Ganges eternal dharma flows.

Wings of Dragon

In this once fabled sacred land
corruption marches with a heroic hand,
it triumphs with a fortified royal face
giving an irreversible blow to ethics
which in dread flees without a trace
or strength to resist the fatal kicks.
In this land looting is a gallant game
shining with a flourishing name;
dragon's wings cover the sub-continent
no field is free from its deadly dent;
the higher you climb the wider the sphere;
the more you rob the more you cheer;
for officials, small or big, all are equal pawns
in their game of chess on table lawns;
the higher the rank the higher the bribe
none can change the colour of the tribe;
the rich, the wretch and the mass
alike like this practice and relish to love;
the poor don't leave their own class
and fleece those who are a step above.
Shameless schools loot parents' anxiety
and rob with a rare scholastic piety.
Our leaders leave no place or field
untouched, they disrobe and rob
with political power, a licensed shield
and a troop of thugs, a hired mob;
let us defend our defence from Bofors,
bullet proof jackets are a big farce;
in the wider field of corruption cricket
a sportive one is always a fallen wicket;
bridges, dams and stadiums collapse,
Governments wink at the cruel lapse,
the wink of our bureaucratic eye scores
and swallows thousands of crores;
inadequate are all the elements five,
not content with the endless grabbing
of land and mines extends their drive
to skies and clouds and rain harvesting;
if these sordid souls are banished to hell

even the underworld they are sure to sell.
Commerce rests on inorganic chemistry
to thrive on pungent fumes and gains,
corruption rests on our ruling ministry
spreads its branches to all lines and drains.
ethics in economics, voiced by Ruskin,
dreads to touch our corrupt bestial skin.

The Fly

I try and try, my hands fail
to arrest its aching trail,
to catch it and stop its flight;
master of fierce guerrilla fight
fast it shoots at my head
helpless without a helmet;
all my skill fails in stead
to avert the impending threat,
in triumph camps my foe
atop my hair with much show
and settles in rare royal gait;
I think of a different strategy
I feel it's better to watch and wait
it is too clever, a real prodigy;
in proud glory it circles and flies,
descends and on my toe it lies;
I can't but admire its heroic tact
and plan to come to a tacit pact;
I resolve now I should not yield,
narrow is the range of battlefield;
my ego bids me to hit the insect
with a pad or broom to bisect;
it harasses with mindlessness
seeing my calm and carelessness;
it curls, whirls and fast it flies
towards my poor blinking eyes,
its moves nagging and persistent
and design of attack consistent;
with pride it moves in rings,
in vain I try to catch its wings;
it feigns to go to the garbage bin
its sudden return makes me grin;
at once I trap it in my happy palm

the little hero struggles and wriggles,
with a smile I let it free and calm.

Blank Script

As a teacher I know the value
of the student's blank answer script
in the examination hall in April,
        blank energy is far from zero.
The answer for Hamlet as a Tragic Hero
is worth a full length book or a thesis
that can't be scribbled in an hour,
        silence reflects a golden mind.
Mind soars beyond ten commandments
restricting the scope and far-reaching vision
of the tested writer of critical times,
        a treasure of unpenned matter.
The unwritten script is a symbolic arch
that opens the gates of unseen tracts and racks
and untrodden realms at the horizon,
        it is a window to see the unseen.
As I gaze and gaze at the milk-white pages
they fill my mind with the matter of ages
traversing countries, cultures and continents,
        it travels beyond worlds.
It soars above the quantum theory
reflects on the painful stretch of thought and time,
merges with Einstein's theory of Relativity,
        it merges with cosmic space.
When unheard melodies are sweet
when unseen beauties are sweeter
blank script with pure pages is greater,
        it travels beyond words.

The Peddler

Once a week he passes by our house
with his rich exhibits of knives of steel
strapped to a board on his whetting wheel;
his jargon tempts men and women to buy
more and more of his shining goods and try;
knives are fresh, rich with wooden handles,
sisters, come and see and buy the new ones,

also bring the old ones to whet and try once';
housewives gather to see the handles,
without a knife life comes to a grinding halt
just as you can't relish food without salt,
without that you can't cut even a potato
or watermelon or apple or tomato;
here knives cut fruits and vegetables,
there they cut throats and lives as cables;
a biker rides and stabs with a knife
fanning the flame of communal strife
cutting peace to pieces in the capital;
to cut meat or a roll of sweet we need,
we lose no time to cut an onion to weep
and soon all the culinary taste to reap;
rightly used it strengthens the span of life
wrongly used it cuts the cord of life;
its invention a mark of civilization
progress from stone age to metal stage;
the peddler pedals his bike old and dry
with the bell ringing his echoing cry.

Hunger

So many mouths full of hunger!
Hunger hungers for food, for rice,
but hands refuse to work in fields,
refuse to plough and plant nurslings
refuse to harvest the ripened crop;
hands have voted the party to power
all the freebies let the Govt. shower;
wringing hands laugh and bring
bags of ground level subsidized rice;
drowned in drums of state liquor
their mouths hunger for more liquor
more bread and rice at zeroed price,
hands holding bottles and sachets
are averse to work in the fields
averse to hold sickle and reap the corn,
but the hands want to reap all benefits,
they cry – poor and penniless we are born,
it is our right to enjoy all free help;
our leaders, who hunger for eternal power

at the cost of all, all freebies shower,
production and progress cry of hunger;
Somewhere, search for real hunger begins
hunger for work and proper pay for work;
then the heart of boiling rice gets freed
from the bad breath and feigned hunger.

Retirement Reality

Superannuated man
cannot run on wheels and rails
or fly with wings all the miles,
his words have lost their flavour
nor his voice do the young savour;
evening walk his only solace
while for others a tedious race;
benches in parks and grounds
invite him to share with his tribe
and see children's games and vibes;
they can't move on wintry days
they shiver like Christmas nights
or helpless leaves in windy storm,
their bones scream for the warm;
Back home they spend their time
with grandchildren that lisp in rhyme
and they too can't spare their hours
as school work drains their powers.
To stand in queue for paltry pension
till they collapse – they can't shun;
they wait at the crowded banks
as college boys at the crowded theatre
to see their fair star's fresh release
leaving classrooms to vacant gloom.
Once his able mind a magic wand
created earthquakes and tornadoes,
now he is slyly ignored and banned,
Frozen in thy heart are volcanoes;
once they were unopposed dictators
now unwanted unwelcome infiltrators;
his word was once an oracle
now it ends as a sad debacle;
Why this reversal? Nature knows!
As roses bloom and Diwalis* sparkle

memory laughs with a faint twinkle;
still his wrinkled wrist has the swing
though his hissing tone loses the ring;
Once he was cheered at his zenith,
now the graph feebly falls beneath;
he breathed out fumes and flames,
now his tongue is dumb, hands numb;
pages of events and feats roll and rally
in his mind's fast shrinking valley.
His ripened moves everyone foils
his memory in distrust faints and fails;
He dies in fact on the day he retires
and resurrects to turn out a new leaf,
faces fresh unpredicted challenges
in this changing retirement landscape,
with tact and skill well he manages
when children find ways to escape;
but now he is too tired to live or die.
To Him his only prayer is to depart
ere his limbs and senses retire to part.

*Diwali is the Festival of Lights celebrated in India in Oct./Nov. with
a barrage of fireworks.

A Broken Statue

It looks so dumb, quiet, still and simple,
though broken-hearted with a broken hand,
lying as a forgotten thing in dusty sand
near the entrance of the ruined temple.
Visitors from far and near to the fort
see the ruined temple and the statue;
eyes full of grace, its marvellous virtue –
all voices echo like judges in a court.
The divine hand that blessed one and all
and the hand that chiselled the masterpiece
faded into dust to rest in tranquil peace;
granite beauty smiles with its eternal call.
While dark cave men found pure joy in art
fanatic hands break the art and its heart.

A Phone Call

Again the phone rings
it brings new things
and binds many strings;
it connects places and persons
countries and continents,
cuts many knots
and umbilical cords;
tense and distance shrink
anxious moments sink,
modern life it rings
glory of the times it sings.
The ring of the phone
when we are terribly alone
is a big welcome relief;
the word, the welcome word
acts as an aerial sword
to kill the devil of loneliness.
The word from the phone
may hit us hard as stone,
still sweet is the tone
the one that we love.
Of late the cell, a real magic,
has become a part of our body,
our basic audible self;
if we forget the cell we feel
the loss of our genetic cell
body feels the missing self.
The ring of the phone
enthrones or invades the throne
defies or delights any zone;
sometimes the ring
is a threat or a thing,
better to avoid the sting.
My eminent friend says
don't buy or keep a cell,
indeed a cell is a hell;
no doubt, it saves your time
but more often it burns
your peace and precious time
and drives you mad with its rhyme;

but it is our reliable friend
a friend in hand, a prop, a crutch,
a light at the tunnel's end
a hi-tech guardian angel
who saves us from deep crisis;
though now and then unknown
it lands us in troubled waters
and the tone stammers, falters,
it drives away the long spell
of silence the terrible arch devil;
a cell makes us bold and calm
with the globe in our palm.

Sweet is Adversity

Sweet are the uses of adversity
It checks the rising foam of prosperity
converts the heart to a crazy rebel
arrests our hilarious mood to revel.
We can't bask in old ways again
we find simple ways strength to gain;
its control of our senses is superb
all research praise thy power in the blurb.
If we fail to follow the strict schedule
and take in time food, pill or capsule,
like an unrefined horse heart beats fast,
so fast that it stops exhausted at last.
If we defy thy threat you turn ruthless,
even insulin our guardian angel fails
to save us from thy fury storming merciless,
no power can save the victim from the grave.
Its magic transforms even urine sweet
entire body becomes a sweet home;
no need to buy and taste sugar or greet,
the fairer foe ensures our burial dome.
Rise of the level of sugar makes us lull,
body becomes giddy, senses pale and dull;
With sagging energy when I try to smile
it smiles like a prowling tiger at my last mile.

In Retrospect

Flying like a winged angel
we can't end up in mid-air
let us stop at ground zero;
prime life in blind heat is lost
in victuals and cultural rituals;
all these rituals, token spokes
in the wheels of social dynamics
now end in dull social stasis;
while individuals and individualities
are fast floating and fading
into Lethe's track of anonymity
terminating all termites of terminology,
why should we burn our time
and our feeble fingers in trying
to find faint fusion in confusion
and evolve a ghost of a formula
from this ever revolving mind;
when I fail to decipher my word
how can I think of probing
into the intricate design of the world
and see the seed of cosmic image
enriched by the divine cosmic music
reverberating the stellar silence
in the maddening cacophony of sounds;
by seeing everything in retrospect,
ruing and ruining all possible prospect
the present loses the trace of respect
and reduces the future to a wreck .
Though the light of the Gita travels
across continents breathing and soaring
breaking barriers and worlds of words
we still roll in the silken sheen of sophistry,
the painted tawdry and IT wizardry;
unless with will power we wisely manage
to come out of this shell of sophistication,
stinking well of ego and false prestige
and the charming wily web of worship
of wealth and power and the wealthy
there is no hope of our liberation
from this self-imposed dark slavery.

After Sixties

Shell-shocked I look aghast
at the blood-stained evening sky,
the land suffers from suicide bombs
and heavy droning of bomb shells.
In my native land my place of birth
I have become oddly outlandish,
I don't know why, I only sigh;
hanging between the razor edges
of compromise and contradiction
life is reduced to a simple pendulum
sighing to stand still in its equilibrium.
After sixties life gets complicated
by getting ungratefully nullified
by regrets and force of remorse,
grief and guilt smarting under
life-long endurance and despair.
The syntax of the moral code
makes it a degree more enigmatic
and leaves me helplessly hanging
in the limbo of incomprehension
blurring the long cherished vision
of complicated angelic arrivals
though belated but deep-rooted
like the stammer of a speaker
that affirms in semantic waves
with the force of Vulcan's hammer
the frozen fluency rooted below;
the cure for these fatal cancers
does not lie in barbiturate prescription,
an overdose gives eternal rest.

Fireworks*

With legion lights the azure sky is ablaze
countless stars descend in pure rapture
the earth's boundless beauty to capture,
these two poor eyes are too small to gaze.
Stocks of fireworks, shot from the ground,
shoot up like sizzling comets into the sky
faster than mythical Ram's arrows they fly
and spread the canopy of light and sound.

Vast aerial space celestial splendour fills
with rainbow colours dancing in circles
like precious stones dazzling in ripples
and the sea of enchanted hearts with thrills.
The old and young celebrate liberty in sunbath,
as balloons fly to kiss the stars on milky path.

* Written on the delightful experience of witnessing the barrage of
blazing fireworks celebrating America's Independence Day on July 4th
at the West Haven beach, CT.

Statue of Liberty

Like a nymph rises from the waves of the ocean
and stands erect on the rock-cut citadel base
the giant awesome Statue with the noble mission
to spread the gospel of Liberty to human race.
With the uplifted hand bearing the blazing torch
and the other holding the book of enlightenment
the new colossus inspires all with a will to march
and reach the goal of equality and its fulfilment.
Pushing the clouds the massive size overwhelms,
An architectural marvel that amazes in any age;
Sense has its fragrant spell on all lands and realms,
Repressed hearts it kindles with hope and courage.
The waves of New York echo the message of light
'Awake, arise! Freedom is your breath and birth right'.

The Hudson

Rising at Lake Tear you wipe human tears
riding fast you march with tidal waters,
proud of your banks with high rise towers
the vast sheet of water blends joys and fears.
Tall oaks, pines and maples sentinels green
guard your course through hills and vales
that echo age old adventures and fairy tales
with cooing thrills of birds of the woody scene.
While cultures and cities rise on your banks
bridges bridge harmony and lend light to life,
and stand on waters to liberate men from strife;
The Liberty Statue in your isle equals all ranks.

While drifting clouds glide in varied forms
the Hudson hugs the Atlantic with her charms.

Buddha

A prince, born and bound to be a King,
chose the path of a sanyasi, an ascetic;
seeing disease, decay and death sizzle
he moved on to solve the baffling puzzle.

He left his wife and child and everything,
in search of truth started his quest mystic;
at last Enlightenment dawned on Siddharta,
the result of penance and made him Buddha.

His pure and simple life worked as a magic,
all castes and classes embraced his path as one;
criminals and cannibals bowed to his logic
and soon hearts of all with kindness he won.

As a great guide he showed the path of Dharma,
to reach Nirvana by treading the Eight-fold path;
for the righteous, no need to be afraid of karma,
The Light of Asia chases evils as greed and wrath.

Unless suffering ends no place for joy or peace,
kindness, not violence, dispels clouds of misery;
compassion strengthens life with a fresh lease,
and in conquering oneself lies the real victory.

In this serene garden of life grief is the weed
polluting Nature's wholesome atmosphere,
and it grows to monstrous size from the seed
of greed, the terrible fire that burns the sphere.

Buddha's message is the huge Bodhi tree
with its root firm in heaven growing free
with widespread branches down on the earth
spreading peace and grace as human breath.

Nothing Follows

This air, this water, this land –
nothing is ours, nothing belongs to us;
Myself I am not, me I don't own,
But everything is mine, ours,
the entire universe is mine,
I pervade the whole Universe
Every atom in me is not mine
but I occupy every atom, every line.
Having eyes we don't see, foresee,
having ears we refuse to hear,
having mind we don't think, we only blink.
This world is a vast stretch of illusion
a fusion of shades, a land of shadows
allergic to touch, explosive to approach;
we run to catch or snatch a mirage
and trust deceit and deceptive glow;
we don't mind to lose our name
and defame the constructed fame;
By the time our charmed eyes open
they are forced to close for ever.
Whole life, packed with plots and blots,
mastering scams and negative arts,
rolls in stink and stench and rots to roots;
no place for righteous act or thought,
no room for the innocent lot;
for the affluent each day a feast,
even a funeral a parade of wealth,
intoxication burns day and night;
for the penury each day ends in misery,
the sun rises and sets in cries of hunger;
Ere this breath stops let us do some good
and feed a handful of starving souls;
this body needs four shoulders or hands
to bear it to the grave, the last journey.
We may win, reign or lose empires
listen to the music of flutes or lyres
and sit on golden thrones with stones,
but our last place is the pit or pyre.
When we come we bring nothing
when we leave we carry nothing,

then why this petty play of heat and hate;
before we depart let us do a bit of good
leaving a trace of fleeting fragrance.

Quest for Peace

(A Minor Social Epic) (N.Delhi, Authors Press, 2013)

1. For this single soul's ceaseless flight
this is a brief linear landing place for rest
to refuel its teasing tank with inherent right,
and refresh with clean air free from pest.
Alas! a loss for the searching soul to rest here,
a stage far from peace, full of foul fear.
This fabled ancient eastern hilly place
relished once the Lord's supreme grace;
Eons ago it was the sacred spot of His choice
on this earth hallowed with His divine voice
that on Gods and humans had cast a spell,
now exiled by the metropolitan pell-mell;
this is now the terrible teeming township
where devils and robbers masses worship,
where unhygienic wily human vultures
making devious efforts without culture
are always busy to their bones as bees
in avidly sucking human blood to the lees
and directing their exhausted energies,
strengthened by wild passing allergies,
soon to deconstruct their cultural remains
on planned ways and sanctioned lines
their homes and old and orphan homes
on the remains of ruins, tombs and domes,
their pieces of lives with missing roots
that are denied optimum growth with fruits –
roots, reduced to remnants and patched rags,
decomposed for export with borrowed tags,
by uprooting broken doors, frames and bones,
cracking walls and roofs and crushed tones,
while a sorely slighted miniscule minority
with positive thoughts full on top priority
coolly venture to reconstruct in a cool way
the rubble and piles of debris and decay

overseeing the artistry of broken images,
the sole inheritance from our ageless sages,
by realigning visual powers of optic lenses
to rewrite the twisted history of three tenses,
rebuild by using recycled wreck in their work
with care lest from devils it suffers havoc
and regain their terrible loss of inheritance,
not the newly acquired one in hot hesitance
with hi-tech layers of corrupt life immense,
and missing peace, robbed amid life intense.
This is the richly reckless feckless sinning city
that lives with the boiling breath of electricity
and the dark stifling clouds of dense smoke
springing round the clock from countless vehicles
racing in high speed spreading the sooty cloak
and rising layers of amorphous dusty particles
that fly and dance before the confounded eyes always
and proudly envelope all the lanes and highways,
constantly made and unmade in fits and starts
with shifting scenes of power in vital parts
with the aid of wounds and wireless words
of chameleon men with hilted whetted swords
where desire and death vie with each other
with equal force the voice of truth to smother.
Alas! All their boasted human conversions
end in mazy mist of mechanical inversions,
increasing global environmental pollution
ending with the chasing ghost of no solution,
with swallowing exploitation by capitalism,
devouring communistic obstructionism,
stinking democracy filled with false visions
crushed under fish-catching reservations,
monstrous increase of contagious corruption
and bribery's ugly face of volcanic eruption,
mindless terrorism spilling pools of blood,
every minute ticking in its streaming flood,
while bridges widen the yawning grisly gulf
wiping out the blooming petals of the self
to lengthen the elastic life of sinful courses
with the hideous help of infernal resources. ...

It is a metro city of fast sinking ships

with atrocities beating the hi-rise towers,
blood of butchered bodies in cruel showers,
mercury of morals to bottom level slips and dips,
crowded bars, rising stars, tempting lips and zips,
fleshy cheeks, pot-like tummies and tuning hips,
parasites showering paeans on pursy powers,
wolves walk in the streets and rest in bowers;,
sprawling with whining dogs and racy rats,
matted pony plaits and crazy cricket bats,
city of burning lights, fights and dark delights
even on cold Christmas naughty nights,
drunken bodies lying on the noisy roads
from dawn to late in the night as toads,
college campuses full of savage ragging,
a sport as common as rape and gagging,
reigning everywhere from remote village
to the civilized Capital with fashion's rage,
a proud place of nocturnal rounds and fairs,
tipsy steps and syllables and gypsy airs,
pitiful sights, nights and pompous pleasures,
limping lazy leisure and pricking pressures,
breath arresting events, and tense moments,
cheering chimes and choking movements,
silent hungers and simmering intensities,
shining parlours and pretty parading beauties,
busy office hours with clerks at tea centres,
retired persons awaiting dues for many winters,
theatres packed with students and wage earners,
mushroom schools as money-minting factories
robbing parents and sucking bread winners,
confused victims their aggrieved votaries,
college teachers always counting arrears
unmindful of students' needs and careers,
public hospitals without doctors or drugs,
Offices full of bribe-breathing bloody bugs
who attend only when we grease their palms
costly beggars awaiting weight of higher alms
legendary foxes waiting at the hollow grave
for the remnants of flesh left by the brave,
roads deaf with ceaseless hi-tech horns,
robes of smoke and stench our city dons. ...
Our tired bodies badly need fresh vitamins

to kill or chill a host of harmful vermins,
these feeble frames need an ounce of strength
or they faint and fall in stupor in full length,
our minds an extra dose of wider study
to scan the nervous moment to be ready
to face any sudden explosive event or trend
or chase the distracting force to the end;
but now they are at the end of bankruptcy
living at the mercy of the tongue's fluency,
mind, closely confined to narrow limits
refuses to budge a whit beyond its petty wits,
sitting in the sea of books it finds itself lost,
books strangely appear as untouchables at last,
our souls ever bankrupt to the cutting edge
leisurely roll in the slimy pool with a wedge,
grope in dark to cross the sinking bridge
like sooty bats winging the vacant space
in broad day light in a futile homely race,
need garlic pearls of morals, more moral pills,
but never a huge laundry list of medical bills,
and words of gratitude, small ethical capsules
to commence in daily doses with rigid rules
and save ourselves, dry and useless bundles,
more often a confusing network of tiny nerves,
for our limping spiritual progress huge hurdles,
from the nervous breakdown at the curves
since our roads and bridges solely rest on sand
and live with the breath of the tiny magic wand.
To survive the nomadic onslaughts of erasures
let us fortify and energize our heart's enclosures.

2. Future is sorely bleak to the cleaner souls,
for every scheme is sour full of black holes;
the present context doesn't need any text,
it knows how to capitalize any tiny pretext;
Those who dream and wish for better days
and the society to tread on clean simple ways
and cherish values of bygone days to flourish
before their eyes see them flee in fear and vanish;
times are too hard for the righteous to cherish
morals on the thorny path where they may perish;
these are the dogged days of cruel commerce,

white collar crime and shameless swollen purse
acquired by sinful means in ways worse,
common man has to bear the hi-tech curse
Our modern leaders fan the dark flame of caste,
a wily weapon to get all the votes, a rich harvest,
a bumper crop full of tall weed, bitter to taste,
a near forbidden fruit in the advanced West;
People of all creeds who lived as loving brothers
during the White Raj now see with hot daggers
in their eyes in this cruelly corrupt native Raj
and follow wily ways to expand their personal Raj;
when any threat they feel to their secure state
or smell some shadowy trace of faint fear
soon to their bright golden royal political fate,
their magic wands release chaos far and near
to divert directional masses from their cause
so as to give some breathing time and pause
and to drive away all fears, threats and losses
and protect their unlawful activities by laws.
Now politics is the dirty game of mechanics
involving dynamites and thermodynamics
in an amalgam of all gases through fusion
and foul fission into an amorphous substance
resulting in an instant explosion of confusion
and chaos, our millennium-old inheritance,
hurling people into an iron trap of illusion
disclosing the horrors of democratic delusion,
hurting the clean progressive sensitive mind
that reflects and revolves over ways to find;
Nation is hurled into a foul and fallen state,
a multiple eclipse foreboding the gloomy fate
darker than in the dingy days of the White Raj
and the pleasure-seeking rulers of the great Taj;
these native leaders in their own way are great
for they ask us to drown all our deep sorrows,
destinies and then our poor selves at a faster rate
at Varanasi where impure the holy Ganges flows;
they have mastered the art of climbing to the top
on multitudes of heads, deprived of reliable prop,
who work as a safe pyramid with a solid base
for the shrewd and selfish few to win the race
with a remote control potential with precision

which is their weird way of political expression;
after all our leaders, blind to the public pulse,
relish to rely on their promoted and grafted purse
always reminding us of our poverty and descent,
not allowing the thought of making an ascent.
Decades of stale impotent and false non-alignment
breeds steady decay and fears of new alignment;
while other nations march in leaps to big evolution
our democratic leaders to insure their voted power
revolve round the axle of worn-out static reservation
through endless populist schemes at every hour;
constant play of this deceptive political game
has rendered our brittle economy horribly tame
and a lion's share of our budget is lost as a whole
mysteriously without a trace in the black hole.
For bumper harvest of votes to ensure power
Governments indulge in cheap tricks to shower
even non-essentials as TVs and laptops as freebies,
to fill the huge deficit break the necks of the bees
by imposing heavy taxes in varied forms and laws
breaking the aching backbones of the middle class;
Governments lift the closed curtains of prohibition
and open the doors of liquor sale with ambition
and let the people drink and drink and drown
till they burn whatever they earn as a clown;
Theatres and liquor shops are overcrowded
while values and ethics are flouted and clouded.
Our local bodies feed on false disinformation
and breed in greed the creed of misinformation,
while our ministers siphon off all the energy
of the common man's sweat and synergy;
Government wings are almost wingless birds,
they never rise, though wise in drafting words;
now and then they seem to move and shine
with borrowed wings, funds and easy wine;.........
Our human rights leaders protest very hot
when extremists and acid killers are shot;
but when citizens and police persons are killed
or with acid bottles college girls are killed
their eyes become blind and their voices dumb,
their human hearts turn blind and minds numb.
Popular ballad singers step in beggar's guise

with pseudo writers to grab land being wise;
these revolutionary self-seekers create unrest,
at the spill of human blood they evade acid test;
hostile to democratic ways they always oppose
constructive steps with a red intellectual pose..........
Gone are the glorious days of media ethics,
now it stinks with foul pranks, pricks and tricks.

3. Hard times collude to fizzle out our will
however hard to withstand do we drill.
Rituals and responsibilities engulf us,
our cruel customs drain and drown us thus,
while senseless ceremonies sing our dirge
and sink in luxury our life's crumbling barge;
In uneasy cohabitation my days I waste
breathing spicy fumes of borrowed taste.
Faith in sheer fear and doubt flies from me
seeing the shy unchanging coward in me;
Faith is as strong as a hard mountain rock
and high as the snow-capped Mt. Everest,
it does not yield for gold or beauty's knock
until it reaches the goal it does not rest;
but the environment with its spell is strong,
like mighty waves it erodes the sandy shore,
it dulls our senses, lures us to go wrong;
the boat of my broken will obeys the rising roar......
I don't want to enter the prohibited field
where fallen angels fear and tremble to tread;
as such I will be happy with a slice of bread;
Governments and their bureaucrats yield
before the proud fabulous private coffers
and their rich tempting golden offers;
Nowadays everything, even education,
is a profitable marketable commodity,
it is simply an open monetary transaction
converting the youth to ethical frigidity;
corporate schools expand their greedy wings,
convert admissions into financial springs,
fleecing sheep and fees is their only aim,
they mint money and marks at any time;
they nip in bud children's creative urge,
for play and joy sing a dragon's dirge,

transform institutes to grim grinding mills
multiplying wily monstrous boarding bills.
They say- 'Sell in the municipal market
our dear private MBA admission concept';
Everything is determined in economic terms
from pins, pens, books, brides and brooms
to foods, goods, brushes and bridegrooms;
A high pedestal now occupy market values
while in ignoble exile go our moral values.
'Win-win market is our dear favourite God,
Profit, pure and soulless, our measuring rod;
bury useless ethics thousand fathoms deep
and get wedded to gold and currency heap.'
Farewell to Sri Ram, Buddha and Christ,
cheers to Satan and his shining descendants
who attract with their rich golden pendants
flying in planes like Ravan in an air of mist;
They are our modern blazing beacon lights
to put out the blinking lamp of our rights
and to show the easy way to earn and earn
till all the hissing wealth hurls us down
into the livid inferno to burn and drown;
In the light of this democratic freedom
we stoop to embrace the teasing serfdom......
We don't have the gorgeous Niagara Falls
to create ravishing rainbows with our calls.
It is cruel to live in this explosive atmosphere
but it is so wherever we go in this sphere;
we have to wander and roam like nomads
till we get exhausted as misdirected lads
until we realize that we are in a hallucination
spread out like a cage throughout the nation.
Our cherished dreams spun with neo-Platonism
may not see the day in this corrupt communism;
we need a revolution, not of borrowed blood
not the narrow theoretical one once magical,
but through clean blood and bone with a flood
of light on sacrifice, a process that is not biological
but related to the mind by tuning the mind aright
with morals in and outside the house or school
from the early days with moral stories right;
these seeds are sure to work as magic tool

and steadily make the mind more ethical
and less selfish, greedy, corrupt and egoistical;
it naturally leads to a healthy collective change
of the rigid mindset to grow to a nobler range
and realize the concept of collective good
where people should work and deserve food
and live in a righteous atmosphere of peace,
and equality, rid of greed and divisive force.
Do we elect leaders to freeze and banish merit
and reserve positions for the rich and residue?
Should we compromise with sheer market spirit
and learn to live with the tainted times and rue?
Then let not the moral spirit in us hibernate,
soon let it rise when people realize and venerate.
This new millennium begins on a positive note,
a clarion call to crush the cruel tyranny's throat;
grit and vision made possible the Arab Spring
chimes of democratic spirit seem soon to ring,
the dictators who ruled for decades feebly fell
and ended in a cage or cave, a cell or a real hell;
the great million march in Cairo at Tahir Square
inspires all as the tragic one at Tiananmen Square,
united voice of the long-suppressed people rises
like a mighty thunder to consume cruel forces.

4. ..... I wish to fly like a bird from tree to tree
and tour the sky with wide wings fully free
and make an aerial survey of land and sea,
woods and mountains as nature's child
which all birds enjoy, even beasts wild,
feel the pulse of fresh breezy morning,
listen to cosmic music and its warning.
Beach is a beach wherever you step or go
native or alien with its bustling human flow –
Chennai or Vizag on the Bay of Bengal,
Kanyakumari on the Indian Ocean's shore
or Mumbai with the Arabian waters regal
where we see a sea of people near the roar.
Once I stepped on the quiet Atlantic beach
within the world's financial Capital's reach;
with sylvan scene it greets at West Haven,
for walkers and veterans a healthy haven;

infant waves ventured to touch my feet
that hesitated to touch the watery sheet;
Looking at the terrible boundless blue expanse
I walked on the smiling sand and shining shells
that lay like fallen leaves at autumn's response
and played with a child with beaded bells
and saw playful waves chasing the tiny ones,
splashed foaming water with my foot at once
and drew diagrams on the damp slate of sand
in pure imitation of the child's restless hand;
Qualified youth thrown on idle Indian roads
like famished birds fly to the American shore,
their revived hearts feel relieved of loads
of fears and tears as hopeful skies they soar;
in the fertile land they try to find fresh roots
and pay homage to the place of fairer fruits;
they find their life and peace in alien skies,
when collapsing economy their balance tries.
When big Lehman brothers, financial giants
and fabulous funding Banks file bankruptcy
heart beat of global economy halts and faints,
even imperial States wriggle in economic epilepsy;
when the sturdy walls of mighty Wall Street crack
even the Great Wall and the Red Fort miss the track.
Already walls of New York face the blasting wreck
when Twin Towers fell to terrorists without a check;
imperial World Trade Centre suddenly crashes
reduced to sky-high flames and chilling ashes
to become a mourning centre of the terrorist act
and Pentagon too shivers under Terrorist pact;
when the land of peace, power, joy and wealth
loses peace with bold terrorist attacks of stealth
how can smaller nations stay and feel secure
when sons of Satan strike with hands impure?
All seasons are richly fertile for corruption
that grows without reason or correction;
For corruption most fertile is Indian soil,
the weed has full growth without any toil;
our 'bribescape' is as vast as the skyscape,
there is no escape route in this landscape;
this holy land dons the avatar of corruption
and shines as world topper sans correction;

Our leader knows there is no magic wand
to cure or end this cancer with a single hand.

5. Corridors of varied experiences are closed,
revised Ten Commandments are imposed;
shutters are drawn on windows of knowledge,
knowledge hubs are rubbed to bankruptcy edge,
known avenues of solutions are dead ends,
party resolutions prove to be dangerous trends
and block the gateway of transformation;
optic lenses face unusual visual aberration,
eardrums suffer constant wear and tear,
they fail to receive acoustic signals fair.
Looking at these multitudes of idle faces
with vainglorious and voluptuous looks
how can we fill in these enigmatic spaces,
empty and unproductive as blank books,
by following without any pause a risky track
with the dubious help of a brainless pack
through the haunting shadow of an invisible trail
where more often we are painfully bound to fail;
the coined poor man with his unpaid debt,
the long accumulated load of liberal loans,
happily received in a series without any rest,
which he revels in liquor though his wife groans
with a parched starving throat every day,
drinks and dances as he would never pay;
the shivering gait of the suffering wife
spreads the stench of her domestic strife
with the aim of replenishing the emptiness
in a room emptied of dust and cleanliness.
At the other end, the metro middle class man
in a single bedroom apartment with no fan
with his old and ever grumbling parents
lives hard struggling to pay monthly rents
and to equip his two school-going children
with sky-high fees and loads of books barren
and a competitive wife with plans too high
with her feet never on earth but in the sky,
tries untiringly to boost his material image
on this relatively still hot youthful page
working in a dictatorial private college

which flourishes fast with fresh foliage
and extracts work from dawn to dusk,
but doesn't want to part even with husk;
the greedy management collects money
beyond proportions as bees suck honey;
to every modern appliance and gadget
he feels attracted, but he knows his budget;
though often he feels strongly attached
soon with an elegant taste he gets detached;
at times he feels jealous of his counterparts
in Government offices full of crafty arts
who hail from a gifted branch of a scoring tribe
whose pay fades before the glittering bribe;
trying to be content with his ordained lot
he spends his days in the cage without a plot;
frigid paleness grows day by day very soon
competing with the autumnal waning moon
and makes him lose the distinction of sorts
between the rising sun and the rising stars.
Though not so good, let us not be bad,
I want to live and move in this sphere
with ethical values in clean atmosphere
with people neither bad nor always sad;
Let us try to make this restless earth
a liveable place of peace, love and mirth.
Before we make unawares our sudden exit,
let us do some good even in small digit;
before it is too late, let us soon awake
or our acts and gestures become fake.

6. Time mocks at our upstart human race,
a dot in this vast immeasurable space;
When regions fight for separate states
pseudo writers open the divisive gates,
pseudo Professors preach lessons of hate
and change the youth to unruly mob irate,
tested unity gets an irrecoverable blow
and harmony bleeds and image falls low;
can there be greater sin or crime or shock
than teacher's misdirecting a tender flock?
When States dispute over land and water,
passions are whipped to burn over matter,

intellects and national interests turn dark,
global spirit our leaders en mass lack.
Borders and martial arts cruelly clash
though in truth both are tainted trash;
hover the clouds of linguistic fascism
and hiss the fangs of regional Nazism,
both hold infernal rounds and dance
and charm minds of masses into trance.
Perverted intellects join to lit the flame,
plot, lead and make slow progress lame,
negative writers bear the vicious torch
to kindle hate and burn in their march.
When lawyers in High Courts turn violent
like street ruffians, justice is sadly silent;
in total silence justice flees to forest
in search of justice and heavenly rest.
Let us obliterate these burning borders,
convert the greedy hearts and hoarders,
power dreamers and power mongers,
power grabbers and filthy foul robbers
who indulge in hate campaign and courses
and let loose divisive and destructive forces;
All these fancied borders are hollow bubbles,
let us break Berlin walls that create troubles
as sons of the supreme God the only Father
by whatever name he is known or called
though in multiple forms He is extolled.
One who preaches hate and kill is no God,
for peace and love stands always true God.
All these races, states, castes and creeds
are man-made lines through savage ages
to perpetuate his pride, power and greed;
let us transcend these limits by stages;
though hard, try to cut the Gordian knot
and remove the dark age-old sinful blot.
When the earth feebly faces global warm
let us act as one to arrest the deadly harm;
If we fail, we will face collective doom,
we cannot be safe in our own rosy room.
Opportunities do not often come and kiss
unless you go and snatch, or you miss.
Prospects have become now terribly dim

even if you go fast to the horizon's brim; ......
we can't predict when the invisible knife
cuts the umbilical cord, the thread of life.
Is it not really bad to wait and think
of travelling alone the last autumnal mile
without a mind to pause, wink or blink
with carnal comforts in stately style?
With knees and joints stiff, old and weak,
all the youthful tastes and tunes I seek;
mass of desires rising in mind always wins
and multiplies my speechless shady sins;
well I know unless I conquer these desires,
I can never purify myself from these fires;
Carnal desires rise like waves in a tempest
and consume my healthy heart like a pest
that destroys the budding grain of rice field
and wrecks the crop from giving rich yield;
when the thrifty hair has turned totally white
if I do not change, to live I have no right,
Well I know my useless days are numbered;
still my heart oscillates to pray for grace
which alone can change my wayward ways,
I moved and lived long with selfish men
with unclean hands and loose tongues
listening to corrupt voices from their den;
Time's razor edge is on my neck and lungs,
give me the last chance to mend or end;
I find neither light nor reason to gloat,
words struggle in vain to cross the throat,
better it is before the Lord to bend and bow,
or I am sure to sink if I fail to repent now;
from these growing sins I can never rise
to see with upright eyes a pure sunrise.
I wish to express my bursting word
before it droops fast feather by feather
and drops vertically as a wingless bird
leaving me alone in freezing weather
at the pale sunset on the edge of night
desperately to rely on the inner sight
which is as elusive as a summer cloud
though I yearn and pray the Lord aloud. .....
Bent on finding peace at the horizon

I go there only to find another horizon
like an expanding ripple after ripple
or like an onion with layer after layer.
In the end, what we feel as a clear end
is only a beginning at the far off bend; ......
My hair is white as cotton without a dye,
I don't want to be a guy worldly wise
Let me remain my simple self till I die
trying to tread the perilous path of truth
though I totter, fall and fail in sooth. ...
The Ganges roars in floods, fumes and flames
and widens its seething sphere to the Thames;
Lord Siva atop the snowy peak raves and rages
in His Sivathandava the dance that blazes.

7. Is search for peace a wild goose chase?
At the horizon can't we find its trace?
Go to the higher roots of the holy Ganges
or to the snow-clad Himalayan ranges,
a dip or a small step will make you shiver,
but you can't get peace in the cold river.
Daily dip or bath may cleanse your skin,
but it fails to nip your wants and vices thin;
where mind is intensely tense in friction
search for peace is a tantalizing fiction;
indeed, peace is a blessed state of mind,
with control and detachment let us find;
one who is content and has peace of mind
in joyous feast and hunger, mirth and death
is the real conqueror of this world blind,
true possessor of all the land and wealth.
True, environment lends energy to peace,
extends its uncertain life with a fresh lease.
In the west or east wherever we go, we face
crime and corruption, wars and riotous ways,
human bombs and bodies with no trace –
foul identity marks of modern human race;
it is tough to stop soulless suicide squads
that relish the ruthless sport of human bombs
as long as there are irrational fanatic guards
who take pride in changing crowds into tombs.
Let us impart liberal moral stories in schools

or we tend to become loose mechanical tools;
not blind fanatical schools where Satan's sons
frame mind-poisoning cold and killing lessons.
Increase language hours in schools and colleges
with ethics and literary fragrance in the pages
from our epics and lives of noble leaders
that can inspire and enlighten the readers;
present dry language skills end in confusion,
only literary taste can lead to moral fusion;
Let Rama, Buddha and Christ be our models
to tread their path with a will without hurdles;
they light the mind with broader outlook
and kindle the flame with spirit of sacrifice;
if children read them in their school book
it inspires their tender minds to banish vice.
Today's children are our wealth and bulwark,
let us guide them with ethics and truth stark.
Where bombs and bullets fail to conquer
a little love will do with a kind generous act
pregnant with power flinty hearts to stir
to bring peace and smiling joy with tact.
In the West, leaves change colours in Fall,
in India leaders change colours in seasons all;
fall colours are the Creator's gift of the season,
here leaders' shifting loyalties, a sign of treason,
though worse than chameleon's changing colour,
shine in misty mythical conscience's flavour;
double speak is their favourite greedy game,
changing parties, indeed an act of sheer shame,
is for them an event of celebration and fame,
a matter of pride in the media to see their name;
it seems we are fit only to be ruled and not to rule,
we kneel before a guy in power, though a fool;
if persons are at the top, wielding soulless power,
people lick their shoes and undue praises shower;
slavery for thousand years under alien yoke
has packed our genes with blind servility;
now real leader, nowhere found, is a big joke;
still our fake leaders with feigned nobility
to curry the favour of Capital king or queen
offer at the central altar bags of cash and gold
and with their names foul with scams unclean

christen all public places and palaces new or old;
multi-million scams is the order of the day
we feel loudly proud of the mystic heights
we have reached in many a cryptic corrupt way,
corruption glowing in spectrums of lights
is our trade mark of developing communication
the mighty hallmark of our flourishing nation.
Mushrooming gangs of petty muscled leaders
from all sundry streets and slummy lanes,
waving hockey sticks, rant like pleaders
and spread their sphere to the capital on planes;
the rich and the poor alike compete in the game
of corruption where both are never slow or lame;
in all classes, corners, layers, and places
exploitation with multiple heads flourishes;
in the eyes of this devil no discrimination
under the sun – go and search any nation;
once the rich exploited the poor and the like,
now the poor exploit the rich and the poor alike;
exploitation differs in its degree and range,
to others the same may look very strange,
it may not conform to your line and length
as long as it has the ingrained strength;
In fact I was born poor, I know the fact
as I was the victim of injustice and wily tact
which spreads its venomous wings to cities
and reigns in academic centres and Universities.
Corruption walks erect with a stout royal gait
and gloried triumph full with many a fatty bait,
like tsunami it swallows every fertile field,
and breaks all barriers and steely shield;
to politics alone its reign does not confine,
of late academic field is its biggest gain;
Universities, where once angels feared to tread,
now invite wolves and foxes to market bread.
Princes and privileges entered history pages,
our elected leaders greedily fill their places,
In the place of kings with crowns and frowns
now strut our leaders in ill-gotten crowns;
with them fast our top bureaucrats compete
in stealthy wealth, racing in concrete heat;.................
These are not the days for Saviours to come,

it is hard for them this terrorism to overcome;
Can there be a more savage event in modern times
than the blasting of Bamiyan Buddha with dynamites?
Hey Buddhaa! *Dharmamsaranamgacchami* !!
Bali bombings shook the island with a heavy toll
while Madrid and London reeled under terror's pall.
The recent shocking terror strike on the Hotel Taj
and Nariman in Mumbai India's financial capital
proves the grisly global power of Satan's raj
and monstrous thirst for blood and life vital;
mindless merciless killing of the lives innocent
reduced metro life to a shivering leaf in storm,
the direct result of the failure of the Government
and Intelligence to scent the alien threat and harm;
when political parties indulge in the bloody game
of shielding terror-striking sections full of flame,
our defenders in poor bullet-proof jackets bleed
and die victims of high level corruption and greed;
the latest attack on Mumbai is a proof, a clear case
of the Centre's all-round failure to check the menace;
a colossal callous unconcern for Nation's security
our Government betrays with growing impunity;
the recent Norwegian Breivik's mass-killing,
a foul horrific act, inhuman and blood-chilling,
is a soulless instance of a perverted mind
with a negative manifesto of a crazy kind.
Even pleasant sports and games are not free
from the venomous hydra-headed terrorist spree;
brave Sri Lankan cricketers have become targets
of senseless terrorists' stealthy rain of bullets;
though the players by a miracle escaped hurt
the attack took human toll with blood in spurt
with scattered bodies in lusty Lahore stadium
the tragic result of devils' monstrous medium;
The latest bomb blast at Delhi High Court
exposes our hollow leaders at the Red Fort,
their parrot words sound too stale and hollow
while their image, if any, falls abysmally low.
Right now the global situation is grim and dark,
throughout the world it is the truth dark and stark;
America runs on the razor's edge of recession,
China on the high tide of arrogance and aggression;

while Japan quivers under tsunamis and quakes
followed by Fukushima crisis of nuclear leaks;
West Asian States in the grip of political shakes,
rising uprisings and bombings without brakes
are yet to breathe the breeze of elusive peace,
for life on the earth no hope of a fresh lease
when the annihilating threat of nuclear war
hangs on nations as a dark cloud of death to mar.
The heart that spread for decades a reign of terror
fell at last, dragged from drain, to kicks and bullets;
the lifeless name rots in a pool of frozen blood
amid public gaze and rage, a furious flood.
People who begin to bask in the Arab spring
may soon feel crushed by winter's cruel sting;
basics of hard fundamentalists are solid rock,
back to zero they are eager to turn the clock;
while India groans under endless corrupt greed,
Egypt bleeds under the violence of a new breed
when a football match transforms the ground
into a senseless violent battle and burial ground;
unless leaders with broader vision take the reins
the pest of the age old dogma kills the brains.
While London's speeding Minister is jailed,
our speeding MLA beats up the cop and is hailed;
our elected leaders within a term amass billions
while their heirs sit on heaps and hills and mines
of corrupt wealth with none to bind their pinions
and enjoy with their minions on tipsy royal lines;
While the poor are denied drugs and medical tablets
our poorer MLAs are gifted with electronic tablets
for their great service in fuelling hate and division
never thinking of the people with any vision;
Here for looting and plundering sky is the limit,
the sphere extends beyond the shores to any digit;
Our top players for their personal records and gains,
betray the nation without any qualms or pains,
once a shock, now quite common is match fixing,
as common as mixing corrupt glasses and betting.
Fate of peace is like a mad man's dress in rags,
in sheer fear and global chaos it limps and lags...........
With the pure ethics in distilled drops of essence
of all denominations of faiths, creeds and breeds

let us cherish a single faith of nobler sense
and sing its glory in sweet flutes of reeds;
before a common faith in peace and love
with a strong fraternal feeling let us bow.
Let us not be narrow and religion-bound,
let us cleanse it till it is globally sound;
religion relates to the past, arrests the path,
while to higher sphere leads spiritual path;
after all religion is a sure step penultimate
to ennoble and lift us to reach the ultimate.
Lord gave us deeper sight, light and rights,
our myopic eyes leave a trail of blighted lights.
This choice land is a strange landing place
for the puzzled groping soul's brief sojourn
soon to fade without a visible face or trace
with a simple inevitable act to bury or burn.
Still, till our last breath let us act and strive
to contribute to the earth to shine alive.
Let us not stand and stare as idle star gazers,
let us move and prove to be true torch bearers,
let us march and burn all vicious forces dark,
on this nobler human mission let us all embark;
let us save this earth from the nuclear bomb
and free this land from human bomb and harm.
Parting ways with greed, let us be wise to rise
and transform this earth into another Paradise.
I love my native land and mother country
with all the defects, limits, woes and poverty;
with a small glowing lamp in my aged hand
I will light up a piece of this clouded land.......
This life is the supreme gift of the One Supreme
to bloom into life divine, not to fade as a bad dream;
What we do shapes our ends on this creative clay,
The Self in us is a mute witness to this mixed play.
Dharmorakshatirakshitah!
Ohm, Santhi! Santhi!! Santhi!!!

Golden Veil

(A Collection of Poems), (N. Delhi, Authors Press, 2016)

The Shell of Solitude

Unused to hawkish hues of dash and drive
I prefer to stay in the sober shell of solitude,
I am forced to wear the veil of cool reserve
and get deprived of the dreamt of touch
of the long-cherished blooming moments;
winds of destiny push me to the stony wall,
I fail to break the wall and I swallow the gall;
cooked up sordid show suddenly blazes fast
to flash and fade in testing times at last;
I fail to cut the tumescent umbilical cord
and free myself from the dark gloomy cell,
I can't expect any help from the seeing Lord
and so there are no cheerful chiming bells.
They say I am from birth shy and timid,
True, I do not know why; now I only sigh;
I can't transform my mute cells, new or old,
Indeed I know now I need to be a bit bold;
Yes, I need the kind rays of the higher Grace,
Bereft of it these lives and lines can't blaze.
Courage often makes a common man a legend
or one has to live and crawl as a lone lizard.

Old Napkins

We old men nowadays are like old napkins
to our fast earning kids and wealthy kith and kin,
trash thrown out as waste and useless tins and pins,
used tissues disposed and dumped in dustbins;
We chide the kids for their odd and erring ways
Their moms shout we the old are cruel always
when they complain their feelings are hurt;
none to feel how our cherished feelings burst.
Children can be free till they do not go astray

Parents should not wink, they should think
Correction at the initial stage is the only way;
If elders fail to advise, children will sink and stink.
When cattle graze in another's rice field
a strong stick does the angry farmer wield;
when leaves and buds are infested by pest,
till pesticides are applied do we simply rest?

Need of the Hour

Thousand years of slavish sluggish timid sleep
after centuries of saga of sacrifices and bloodshed
ended at last with our flag flying free and high
only to see our corrupt forces hoisting selfish agenda
with their corrupt flag flying high on Mt. Everest.
When everyone vies to be clever and mighty
innocence has lost all the revered sense and sheen;
it is the pale signature of the ineffectual angel,
a mute witness to the unlawful cabal's cruel cudgel.
When leaders buy caste, communal and reserved votes
with their corrupt sacks of wealth to see it multiply
rapes and acid throws are the youth's cranky craze,
from top to bottom offices stoutly stink with stench,
law makers are our law breakers to suit their ends;
Bad elements reign and are always on the spree,
their forces kill, chill and thrill and are fully free.
Here one who lives on honest means is a born fool;
Only those who hate and cheat, grab and rob rule,
robber kings reign in royal robes and crazy crowns,
while pseudo-scholars shine in convocation gowns,
powers at the centre thrive in shearing and sharing;
While the righteous have lost confidence and courage
anarchic forces are freely let loose with riotous rage
by power-hungry political parties, rotten to the core,
who play devil's game to divide the unbiased people
on elusive lines of caste and creed, breed and zone
by burying ethical frame of mind and spiritualism
by the new found weapon of pseudo-secularism.
We eagerly look to a true leader with a clean wand
to save this most abused and misused ancient land;
another avatar of Narasimha is the need of the hour
to establish dharma and end corrupt secular power.

Choose the Right Path

My travel continues from dawn to noon
No shade; I walk in severe scorching heat
It is not the end, I hope to reach it soon.
As throat dries up, reluctant are my feet.
The sun is on my head at the foot of the hill
Beneath the peepal tree I stand, I stare at the split,
The path splits in two, my tired feet stand still;
Which path I should choose is above my simple wit.
Mind is the veiled mischief maker, a breeding field
of worms and wasps, owls and fowls and seeds of weeds,
drives us to the ravishing rainbow colours in lust and greed,
makes us shrink and shiver from higher goals and needs.
To the easy one, the pleasant cosy one, mind leads,
instant fruits and sweet comforts it dreams to reap;
Mind is averse to austere steps as in pain it bleeds,
It runs to seek all pleasures and treasures in one leap.
The branching into two hostile ends I watch with a will –
One seems smooth and safe, leads to majestic metro lights,
the other a zigzag climbing track up the winding craggy hill;
One, a feast of festive lights teeming with tempting sights,
the other, a hard and arduous climb through haunting nights.
Mind tempts me to sail through the warping windy way,
Inner voice urges me to climb higher above this clay;
Search for Truth, an uphill task, leads to lasting bliss,
We are not sheep to graze and relish ephemeral kiss.

A Bird in the Cage

Who said – A bird in a cage is worth two in the bush?
Well, it is an outdated putrid prescription
The truth is – a thousand or more in a cage
can't equal one that flies in the sky in any age;
From bough to bough it flies singing free
from wood to wood, from tree to tree;
It tours the sky in sheer joy and flaps its wings,
in multiple ways it flies in delight in aerial rings.
With the gently blowing wind it flies and floats
Over its aerial survey of the land and sky it gloats

In search of grains and ripe ears it moves on fields
In spotting grain the power of the eyes it wields.
Poor pigeon in the metallic cage in a corner pines
Looks at the fellows of its tribe flying free and high
Watches the dog in the street that runs and whines
The little bird can't flap its wings; too tiny is its sky.
It sings, not with full-throated thrill and joyous ease
It wails and groans like Egyptian slaves in Pyramid days
With blocks to sing and walls to wing it pines for peace
and waits with searching eyes for better days and ways.
Like prisoners in the cells of the white Andaman Isles
the captive bird pines all day and night full of dreams
of unrestricted flight in sunny skies for miles and miles
her songs at low tide turn out to be poor sickly screams.

Meaning of Love

Changing shades and contours of love
are beyond the brush and the word
Sometimes heart may seize the spark
it flicks, clicks and in a wink it slips and skips.
The word love is a complex thing
Who can describe or define or draw it?
It defies all; it is beyond our comprehension
because it is a hypothetical impression
to some it looks as a hypocritical version
Verily an amazing, dazzling expression
Of course it is a baffling mystic concept;
At that level it is good to accept.
If I try to probe or go deep into it,
days, and nights and years we may burn,
Still its total meaning we can't learn.
When we begin to think of love
days and nights may roll unknown
seas may sink, stars may recede
the sun and the moon may get eclipsed;
The encircling embrace of the lady love
may imprison in the ecstasy of the moment;
Later feeling free we are in the thick jungle
of the confusing mazy mass of meanings
which push us nearer to the mark of love,
but not to the point of white splendour

amid dark and dense clogging misty clouds;
too heavy a dose of obsession may push us
to the baffling brink of cerebral break
or as a prize possession of the lunatic zone;
It is pure and lucid for one who is pure at heart
It is shady or awry for one with veiled art.
Where mind takes sides clean heart knows
It knows where the stream of true love flows.

Tell Me What He is!

Most men think they are highly decent
May be an impression of the sprinkle of scent
on their dress of John Peter or Arrow mark
or the luxury car the cynosure of all eyes
in shallow society relishing the feast of lies;
They feel real estate makes them look decent,
khadi dress or gold chain may be the reason,
land or yellow gold shines even in a dry season;
They are not gentle ladies to shine with jetting hips
or quixotic cuts on back blouse or with painted lips
or varied modes of measured walk or honeyed talk;
He rants in the echoing room, vain voice zooms,
he can't be cool or calm, thinks we are fools;
He proudly wants others to swarm around him
and sing choric paeans like humming bees
but we are not little bees to hang on to trees;
He thinks there is fire and flame in his eyes,
though they are not sparks but foolish flies;
there is magic in his dearer khaddar he thinks,
though beyond scented measure it stinks;
A victim of insatiable thirst for power and wealth
he winks at our basic needs with looks of stealth;
in the tick of his watch, in the click of his wrist,
in the jerk of his neck or waist or lip's twist,
in the grin of the chin or in his casual ride
there is the arrogant mark of bubbling pride;
In every sense it makes us sick. Tell me what he is!

Water is Dearer than Blood

Blood is thicker than water, they say
It may be thick or thin, it is not my kin;

in fact it is not my concern right now.
I am thirsty of water, not blood, never.
Here in my land water is dearer than blood;
in this rainless land, haunted by drought,
water is a rarity, rain a rare spectacle;
unless we drill a thousand feet deep
we can't dream of getting a drinking drop;
of late more often it proves a losing gamble,
an abortive step throwing in economic shambles;
Deceptive clouds of election promises don't rain,
let drops of honesty wash our myopic minds
and ease our hearts and cleanse our corrupt hands.
Clouds may fly and ride over our scorched heads,
they may rave and rant as savages, race and reign,
but with empty burning bellies they don't rain.
Village is hard-hit with lack of water, lack of order;
thrown in the tiger's grinding jaws of factions,
bastards born of dirty elections and petty politics,
words and acts lead to clashes that spill pools of blood;
they spread cold wars with cold blood that yields
not a drop of water but only hate and heat it breeds;
Road to water leads to life, not to pools of blood,
road to life lies in peace and smiles, not in lies.

Syntax of Love

Love is the key to soften the clouds
and shower recharging smiles as rain
to analyze the complex structure
of the woven threads of subtle life,
of letters that breathe meaning
and bind and pack all flavours within;
Locked letters and sealed lips
open and glide together united as one.
The unforgettable day we met
your soft sealed lips did quiver
eyes shone with white sheen
glowing with the mute message
of trust and truth, the syntax of love.
Looks are not simple listless looks
but profound ravishing virgin books
with the enchanting calligraphy
of ceaseless flow of celestial kisses,

fragrant petals of milk-white jasmines;
your serene smile tunes the sweet lyre
of the syntax of our conjugal life,
Visual prints far excel finger prints
Our blood is the best judge and witness
We know we are born for each other
Our hearts quietly merge into one
and transform two sunny streams
two clauses, two destined causes
to one crystal clear symphonic stream
to one pellucid simple sentence
with bliss in life as the only goal
with the finishing touch of a divine dot.

Unmask Thy Veil

Now we are together
Tell me dear, my heart and breath
What is it that pricks your noble mind?
Don't feel lonely or shy or sick at heart
Disclose me the cause, that smarting part
undisclosed till now even to thy parents
for reasons, if any, best known only to you;
What you may not generally like to share
with others, close inmates and intimates,
tell me here and now and unburden yourself.
I feel thy painful pulse and heart-beat
Trust me and let us be on our naked feet
Unmask thy veil to break thy walls and wails
Break thy reserve and dubious hide and seek.
Indeed our self is hidden by an ignorant veil
It is not easy to tear it and get the release;
Dark and dubious is the veil, the foe of fulgent light
Its scope is narrow, it blurs the real vision
Vicious is the veil, need of the hour is truth
With will let us free our self from the veil
and try to seek the Truth behind the veil
Ultimate Truth lies beyond the golden veil.

Let Me Stand Erect

Neighbours wish to see me fall and fade
In fact in their hearts they kick me out

Though through troubled waters I wade
and keep quiet as a cat, still they shout
To clean clothes I climb hard from stitches
Still I fall a victim to the evil eyes of witches
My life is simple with hard-earned bread
and I like to share these slices with others
but my neighbours burn with a heavy tread
The designated dons are in no way good
they can't relish to see my work or its worth
The more they ignore the stronger is my will
None can change the course of stars at birth
In higher centres of learning malice reigns still
Envious fangs raise their hissing hood to strike
and wait on pins to hurl me in academic gloom
They feel terribly sore when me my students like
When they wish my doom, by God's will I bloom
When they long to see my quill and will broken
I move and march with an unruffled mind unbroken
I neither gloat, nor feel proud nor get depressed
I prefer to be cool and calm, simple and fire-proof
I like my likes and needs to be more compressed
They say I am reticent; I like to be gentle and aloof.
From patches of thatch quietly I march to stand
Stormy winds of stress and strain I withstand
From pensive past rooted in pain and penury
I march through varied shades and scars of injury;
From the clouds of rage and envy I emerge like a star,
Let me stand erect and soar upright and fly afar;
Soaring above the clouds of regrets and total neglect
I hope to leave a few humble lyrical notes to recollect.

Sylvan Scene

Lucid stream hops from the slopes of nearby hills
and flows speeding to the thirsty greeting plains
as a lively bird that flies care-free from tree to tree
while all the land and the air its musical voice fills.
Filling pit and pond across the path the stream marches
dancing as a sprightly girl through creeping leafy arches;
As a rare boon from bounteous Nature graceful for ages
it travels by our little colony dotted with a few cottages.
Music of the rustling leaves and flowers chases forces dark,
Bewitching beauty, green and serene, is its majestic mark;

Waters clean and crystal-clear run on stones and pebbles,
with the grace of a swan it glides in ripples through bubbles.
Trees tall and stout stand as constant sentinels loyal
in green robes that surely rob our robust hearts royal
on the sloping banks of the flowing pond and stream;
We feel we are in a thick forest or in an Elysian dream.
Studded with countless rubies and sapphires of flowers
and plants as a priceless necklace banks dazzle the eye;
Roses, tulips and flowers of purple and yellow colours
enthral the hearts of thousands that watch and vie.
These enchanting flowers with the wafting breeze
dance as tribal children with pearls of blooming faces
from above the ground and atop the boughs of trees
to the melodic tunes of water that glides and races.
Sparrows and pigeons clap and flap their smiling wings,
Their chirping and humming notes echo in happy rings;
Yonder the crescent moon peeps from the golden sky
to breathe this ravishing bliss from the space so high.
Long after rinsing the golden glory of the sylvan scene
its balmy beauty lives in mind with its emerald green.

Riverside

Let us hurry up to go to the riverside
Decades later it is full with flood water
Long bank looks like a slimy snake or rope
We can't wait; it may dry sooner or later
We may not live to see such a scene again
For years and years hardly does it rain
The sun hides behind the western hills
Tender twilight kisses the barren land
that shines with a soft glow and thrills
Waters with mellowed music move and glide.
Stars stand above to gaze and greet the moon
Let us walk and feel the kiss of the breeze
Moonlight hugs all the land very soon
as tired birds reach their familiar trees.
Ah, my love, the bank is bright with light
It is cool and clear as a mother's heart
No longer can we walk, it is night
Duty calls us back as living is an art.

Our Thirsty Land

A land girdled by hills and woods
crescent-shaped range of hills
green cover of woods with changing moods
sometimes green and often a shaven beard
Larger part of the hills bare and bald
full of rocks and rocks, granite blocks.
Sight of rainfall is a rare event of joy
More often clouds visit, but they refuse to rain
Rain for days in torrents is a dream in pensive pain
Rarely it rains; when it rains it flows and goes
No storage tank or lake or ponds or canals;
years of drought – only record in our annals;
For a pot of water we run too long
chasing the distance with a folk song.
Expecting rains we plant groundnut seeds;
with no hope of clouds, the seeded land
turns for the betrayed seeds into a burial land;
We are regular victims of heat and hot waves
and total aliens to foggy morns and cold winds,
to freezing kisses of the northern snow-clad peaks;
No sincere scheme, no clean framework to develop
We continue to be drought and hunger-hit;
People at the top and bottom reap all fruits,
those in the middle bear all the breaking weight ;
With no hope to rise, they weep and bleed
Small farmers are reduced to hungry coolies
They are forced to sell their patch of land,
sure, a temporary gain, or leave their place
in search of green pastures to feed the flock.
Rain, rain, humbly we pray you not to go away
Please do not wait to come another day.
We cry and die for a drop of rain like chakora
to feed our children; let not our prayers go in vain.

Ultimate End (A Sonnet)

Oblivious of our time limit like proud tyrant kings
on unbridled horses of desires humans want to ride
to roll in earthly comforts and enjoy sensual things
With corrupt wealth they stride in swelling pride.
They don't hesitate to kill and thrill and spill the blood

Unopposed they wish to march on blood-stained soil
As eagles they try to invade the skies above the mud
Used to fuss and fraud, they laugh at those who toil.
Ever hungry to rule and roast riding on ceaseless lust
They march in arrogant ride under the furious sun
They forget the truth of the ultimate end in the dust
where all beings, from man to mosquito, unite as one.
Is it not shame to yield to fleeting dazzling bubbles
and to reap heaps of sins and court unseen troubles?

To Rest in Peace (*A Sonnet*)

The setting sun looks weak and yellow bent too low
He shines before he sinks in his last glow to fade;
As soon as the fast failing feet of twilight sink below
Darkness waits as a quiet prowling wolf to invade.
The moment breath stops there is the endless silence
All the power of mind or sceptre can't revive the breath
From the fatal moment there is no escape, no defence.
At the final call none can resist the clasp of cold death.
On the stage we move as toys, players in a masquerade
With all gibing jeers and gestures we strut on the stage
When Time tolls none can cross the line of barricade
From the unseen book of life, torn is the last pitiful page.
Life is a race, rough and tough; let us move with grace
Let us dream and die, die and dream to rest in peace.

Eden Garden

Near the ancient temple round the park
with children I go for evening walk.
The little ones run inside in a smiling race
The curious eyes do not rest on one place.
Park stretches on two sides of the small rill
During rains water comes from the nearby hill.
Hills with protected trees stand a walk away
In severe sun beneath the trees they sit or play.
The western hills feel the parting kiss of the sun
We, the aged, sit on the old wooden bench;
Children are busy in their play and flawless fun
while I look at the flowers and the fairer bunch.
Children play with ball and bloom as flowers
clapping their hands at the sprinkling showers;

Their smiles are pearls and pretty lotus petals
For a brief while we forget we are mortals.
It is a small pretty park, an Eden garden
A Paradise for the pure minds of children;
They are not the children of the fallen pair
They are the sparks of the One Eternal Sire.
They are here to taste the lasting spiritual fruits
and make this land a Paradise with our divine roots.
Children bounce and play free from grown up spite
Garden grows and smiles when our ways are right.

This Fragile Body

I know I am reasonably old
Truth is no one likes to become old
But it is a thing that can't be avoided;
Like everyone else I too wish to be young,
young in mind, young in bone and tone;
The latter is beyond my human reach
So with gritty will I can reach the former
I can obliterate lines of physical objections
and cross the barriers across the path
and reach mind's fastidious inner court
crowded with hopes, regrets and images
that ultimately leave me in a black hole
where I struggle stupefied and dazed
perplexed to the farthest end of the hair
in derecognizing the more imagined prospect
in retrograde march with retrospective effect,
and in deconstructing the designed Paradise
but the elusive non-descript present prescribes
prohibited drugs and pills for incurable ills.
For a brief while, mind likes to wander as a monkey
in the marshy wilderness and jungles of jugglery
darkened by vague smudges of perpetual guilt;
Mind is now fed up with old generalizations
the lulling legacy of dusty and rusty generations.
Need of the moment is neither figment nor pigment
but some fitment formula to satisfy a segment at least;
Now it wants moments and momentous events,
it craves for memories of erased images of the past
of faded shades and graded and traded shadows
dumped in the drain of the subtle subconscious

without an expressive point or vivid pointed focus
except the feeling that so many years have rotted by;
Neither a re-reading of the old worn out tales and tracks
nor the auditing of the past sweets and scars will do;
Previous deletions, concessions and obsolete obsessions
lose their warily borrowed loosely hanging awful identity
in this kinetic moment of thermodynamic present;
What matters now is the now and this moment.
How long should I bear this enforced estrangement
in my house, in my land, the place of my birth and being;
Past has deluded while the future seems to elude.
I do not like to be crushed between Scylla and Charybdis
and I wish to stand firmly on the rock of the present
and chisel an eye-arresting statue of my bleeding self
my insignificant self without any identity on this stone.
Adieu to the ancient mysteries, mistakes and miracles;
All my experience over the years bursts as a bubble
if it fails to recharge and illuminate the crux of the now;
Then let this fragile unremarkable perishable body
dissolve in the unsolved mystery of five elements.

My Father's School Days

My father often recounted his school days:
With a tiny towel around the toiling waist
sweating in the hot sun he sat as a mild lad,
the brown skin assumed a shade, not so bad;
Semi-naked children played with bare feet,
their bodies bare as earth in the slapping heat
of the malicious scorching mid-March sun
on the sand-carpeted ground with all the fun
beneath the wider wings of the tamarind tree
in front of the village teacher's hut with spree.
It was an open school beside an earthen street,
where cows would low and sheep would bleat
under the open sky that served as school vault.
On the slate of sand carpet for hours without a halt
they practiced their alphabets and perfected the art
with their pointed forefingers tasting burning pain,
and mastered tables and moral verses with their heart,
with one-mindedness they did for their future gain;
When the teacher went inside the thatched hut
pupils were left free to play with a sportive cut

oblivious of the caning of the orthodox teacher
whose presence united sternness and silence,
tender care and love of a mother and preacher
and hushed communion free from any violence.
The lines they learnt stayed alive till their end
and shone unstained by the wily modern trend.

Jai Jawan

How long could she wait at the depressed door
Her boundless patience could wait no more,
Though strong as a rock it melts at a steady run
her joy recedes and dissolves at each setting sun
The day he comes is indeed a merry festival of lights;
Once a year or so he comes with year-long dreams
on leave granted for a month or so with all the rights;
When he comes her eyes gleam and light streams
Her cheeks shine as apples with the sunrise glow
Her heart reflects sunset's tranquil golden glow
His coming arrests the rising tide of her heaving sighs
The cloud of enveloping gloom feels shy; away it flies;
His presence blows out the cobwebs on her chest
Lonely nights now seek conjugal joy and sweet rest
She feels the lingering warmth of the transporting kiss
Joy of every moment of his stay she does not miss.
Her smiling face now glows with the rising golden disc
her mind is quick and free from traces of imagined risk;
An urgent call from the centre, no time to think of fears
The next day he left with a parting kiss to his wife in tears.
A week later while her mind was still sailing high
with his smiles and sweet kisses in the moonlit sky,
the word came – He fought like a hero till the end
Till the last moment his valiant spirit would not bend
His racing bullets swiftly killed ten before he fell
to the bullet of a terrorist, which none could smell;
The next day his body would fly from the border cold
and reach this remote village in State honours bold.

Today's Rural Life

Here farmers look at the skies
Their bowed heads heave endless sighs
Our fields how can we cultivate?

Heat and hunger our hearts can't calibrate
When can we see our fields green ?
Cows, bulls and sheep move feeble and lean
Ponds, tanks and wells die with thirst
for a spell of long-awaited rain to burst;
As rains recede, their area terribly shrinks
as land grabbers grab with political links;
Streams and canals where we learned to swim
have lost their address, now they don't exist;
Both sides are annexed; picture is dim;
Big landlords, political wigs, whips and thugs
and reserved persons none can resist;
We, the marginal farmers now fail and fall
At the dry well or the mocking margin wall;
Unable to feed the cattle, them they sell
to metro kalebas; for the dumb, a real hell.
With fields barren and dry, they turn to cows
With cows the only source, their life glows;
For power-mongers their vision is on vote harvest
If farmers live they live by selling their land
With water, power and labour rates sky-high
farming drowns us in debt and death well nigh;
Can we ever breathe the rich harvest breeze,
Can we ever see the good olden days with ease.

Green Canopy *(A Sonnet)*

Tired of the din and dance I seek the shelter of the wood
With joy I flee from the greedy mass of the concrete jungle
from deafening sounds and smells of spicy juicy junk food
and from lolling tongue, tolling speed and ringing jingle.
For a day from morn till the spent up sun to spend unseen
walking on the leafy banks of forest brooks is my dire need;
Relishing the tunes of birds with eager aesthetic sense keen
and sitting on the roots sipping green bounty is bliss indeed.
The wide sloping rock on the hillside lures our curious eyes,
Canopied shelter of the age-old trees guards the granite rock;
It greets all to rest on its naked breast and forget their sighs;
How long I lie I can't say; green gold arrests the flow of clock.
Mind, sunk in the chaotic crowd, shrinks and moves too slow
On the quiet green bough koel's evening song gains the glow.

The Middle class Man

How long should I bend and bow
to these proud unscrupulous political thugs
and corrupt bulging bureaucratic bugs;
Though, not to bow I had taken the vow,
the system is such, all in all are these bugs;
the more we despise the more they suck,
squeeze and suck and hoard stealthy wealth;
I enter their dens and come out half-dead;
The more you kick the higher as a ball I rise
till you really reel and feel foul and fall sick
You think you can outwit being slippery wise
The dust it raises envelopes you and your eyes
The day is not away, you have to pay the price;
I am a common man of the slighted middle class
Our class is hurt and hurled into the grinding jaws
of the devil's system, the grip of tiger's claws;
Classes above and below reap all the fairer fruits
while we in the middle are crushed to the roots;
We the vast majority, ignored, bear the brunt and pain
In this dangerous democracy, small numbers always gain;
With heads lowered our spirits are badly broken;
Even lip sympathy is not there as a token gesture.
Teach us the subtle art and craft of early rising
without shedding a drop of blood in uprising;
I am a drop, I am the tide, turbulent and hungry,
riding on the crest of cries of wounded time;
I hope to reach the other side one day or other;
System, rotten to the core, blocks my way, my rise;
I, an atom, am sure to explode and blast this rot
and see a wholesome change and general rise.
I rise from the thatched and patched humble hut,
I rise from the bleeding wreck and riotous rut
My arms and bones are broken bamboos
My mind resists with will to sink in the blues
I am the shining spark of the Supreme Lord
I shall tear the thwarting veil like a leopard
These forces dark can't arrest my marching step
From freedom's abuses let us steer clear
to bring a healthy ethical change without fear.
Let us toll the knell of damned dynastic rule,

In every field an iron mace these rioters wield;
Time it is to open our eyes and cease to be fools,
Our conduct, clean and non-corrupt, is our shield.

Erstwhile Farmer

Beneath the tamarind trees tall and stout
a few huts of mud walls with thatched roof
rise as signs of erstwhile simple rural life,
they stand for life in olden days in hamlets;
palm or coconut fronds tied with bamboo sticks
act as a token boundary wall or fence,
a poor man's natural course of defence.
Ample place is left in front and kept clean,
Huts with mud walls and mud flooring
shine with clean and healthy cow dung coat
Hut is built with neither cement nor brick
With mud it is so smart with the right click;
Men relish open bath under the neem tree
On that limited water the little garden lives free
A pandal strong stands in the front vacant space
and holds hay stack to feed his pair of bulls
that plough his field dry or wet in fast pace
The cart of his family like a lusty bull he pulls
With his pair of bulls he goes to field at sunrise
His spouse brings for his breakfast water-soaked rice
his usual healthy stuff heavy with mango pickle
the right combination for the tongue to tickle;
Like a bull with the bulls he toils hard till noon
Full of sweat at the vertical sun he returns soon
Finishing the routine ritual of simple midday meal
of ragi ball with *gongura* chutney, tired he does feel
and for a while his wearied limbs stretch on the cot;
Soon he runs to guard the field from stray cattle
and with the spade to cut the weed to the root to rot;
At dusk with his bulls he returns as their bells rattle
After the bath and night meal, and a brief talk
his tired limbs after the daylong toil fall asleep
on the hard threaded cot of old wooden stock;
His spouse closes the door for the day to sleep.

Seeded Soil

Like the sinking words of a dying man
Deep sighs of the seeded field sadly span
Wheel of Time turns a full four week
Groundnut seeds sown turn too weak.
Like a stealthy sheep strays a cunning cloud
flees scared of sun's fury with a face bowed
In vain go farmers' solemn prayers for the rain
In the furrowed field groans the betrayed grain.
A few seedlings dare to rise and see the light
Soon sun-burnt the shoots fall into dusty night
A rainy drop can wake and make them breathe
Beneath the soil seeds lie buried with the sheath.
Poor farmers' dreams and seasonal hopes tall
as boats in storm sink and face the wreck and fall;
Drowned in woes and caught in dreaded debt trap
they see no way save to sell the land their only sap.

Learning is Life

Life is the greatest teacher, we know
Life is the greatest school beyond all norms
From cradle to the last breath we learn
As long as the will to learn stays we learn
The trinity of earth, sun and moon and stars
transmit their eternal message in natural ways
Day and night with light and dark protect us
The world is an awesome zoo, vast and wide
As observers, let us look at this amazing globe
and learn from tree and leaf, fruit and flower,
from ant to elephant, dog to deer and lion
from crow to cow, reptile to fish let us learn
Form all the five prime elements of nature
fire, air, earth, water and sky let us learn
Each has a clear message, no hide-and-seek
Noble ideas let us seek and receive from all
Let us view with equal vision all dualities
joy and grief, heat and cold, fame and shame,
Let us be content simply with what we get.
Let us not expect high; it leads to despair
One who has created us created all
His creation can never be a waste

though it may not suit our limited taste
What we truly deserve we get, no more no less
God doesn't interfere, He is an Observer
It is karma that shapes our means and ends
Let us learn and receive the good from all
to guide us to right path to save all from fall.

Ego

At the heart of the wilful word
          centre of the sizzling sword
in the cells of the boiling blood
          drop of the tidal flood
in the pitiless leap of the leopard
          lean line of the boasting bard
          obscene look of the lusty lord
reigns the wrecking power of ego.
Beyond the power of ink
          the circle of stink
          the range of think
deep in endless ego we sink.
We feel we are the supreme lords
swell with the songs of slavish bards
live in the world like fools and frogs;
Neck-deep in the Serbonian bog
we sink in abyss like rocks and logs.
Till we are freed from the iron grip of ego
the veil that makes us wail and fight
we stay in dark away from the strength of light
Peace and bliss of light till then we forego.

Listen to our Song

Listen to the painful pulse of the peasant,
the burning beat of the farmer's heart,
rhythmic sighs of the wearied weaver,
storming wails of the famished fisherman,
spinning sorrows of the reeling potter,
burning anguish of the heaving blacksmith,
moaning breath of the sighing middle class
at the soaring prices and sky-high cost
from morn till night in all seasons of the year,
painful cries of fainting school children
collapsing with heavy bags of bulky books,

starving cries of cows and sheep for green grass,
mute mournings of bleeding red sanders trees
felled without a pause at the Lord's sacred feet;
Listen to the music of our great National song
that sings of the riches of our land, wide and long
and makes us stoutly feel perennially proud
and sing in tunes the memorable song aloud;
The day we got our freedom from alien yoke
we lost liberty crushed under the corrupt yoke.

Longing for Rest

At the Sunday evening smiles the moon
who wants to spread his milky light soon
I stand in sweat facing the mellowed sun
After the hard race from dawn I can't run.
I wish to see the golden rays of the sunset
vibrant sounds of the flapping wings at the nest,
faint lowing of the cattle returning to their pegs
cows hurrying to their calves with tired legs.
I have travelled without pause or rest too long
My heart faints after too many gasping miles
I need a little rest, still confused thoughts throng
I am deprived of the power of those recharging smiles.

Calmness glides in ripples at the temple bell
All fire and burning fury spent, the sun would set
All the chronic ills bells ring out and bid farewell
After this long fret and fatigue I long to lie in rest.

Grow Old We Must

Like it or not we grow old, here all grow old
Though not now, tomorrow meet we must
This inevitable encounter let us face it bold
Better with grit greet it and taste it as a crust
Let us embrace it as a lover warm, not cold.
Flowers or leaves can't stay in constant bloom
The sun cannot stay always right on our head
Plants and petals face the change giving room
Earth, moon and planets in fixed orbits tread
Nature's law we must accept till the day of doom.
Beauty, only skin deep, fades after a stage

Glory we lose which we often fail to keep
Strength we lose, it goes with the greying age
But for spiritual growth it is a welcome leap
We are born to die, so why should we weep?
Younger dreams and cherished goals soon disappear
Heart with unrealized dreams often alone weeps
Light of ideals fades from eyes bare and clear
Soon chastened mind with ripened age creeps
Power and glory pale before an act that wipes a tear.
Old age has its honour with all its wrinkles unkempt
Geriatric gains and old age privileges cease to tempt
If mundane mirages fade Truth tries to shine aglow
All passion spent, mellowed mind moves sober and slow
with rainbow charm it has the soft sunset glow.

Waiting for an Avatar

Moves and moves frantically inside the cage
the hapless parrot struggles at a tender age
Though not now, later it would be left free
It can't be held any longer as a poor captive
Time is ripe, it knows the moment has come.
For a full thousand years we were bonded slaves
When the truth forced itself into their minds
they could no longer hold us in their iron grip
They let us at last free, to fly free, to fight free.
The veil of ancient innocence is torn to pieces
Blood group varies, lines crisscross, anarchy reigns.
The upright lose faith, the corrupt snatch all the gains;
Equations of caste and colour, tongue, creed and breed,
and power-grabbing schemes decide the blind directions
while dynastic domination is the villain of the piece;
they spread anarchy, play havoc in all spheres of life;
Real leaders live unknown and merit is strangled to death.
Thousand vicious years of enforced slavish yogic sleep
in bestial bondage under the despotic ruthless alien yoke
has transformed us into a toothless spineless indolent race,
a bowing race of labouring sloth and servile surrender.
Let us await a true leader, free from vicious greed
with the spirit of sacrifice for the nation to be strong
to wake up the nation from snares and nightmares
and drive out the dark negative forces as the rising sun.
Unless the Unmanifest manifests His Supreme Self

on this blood-soaking and sobbing oppressed earth
no common mortal can save this stinking bleeding land;
Let us wait for the arrival of a fresh Ugra Narasimha
or another righteous Rama with axe or the unfailing arrow
or the Almighty Krishna with His countless forms and means
to counter the countless terrors, scams and schemes.

Watching the Field at Night

How pleasant is this wide stubble field,
white and yellow spread with shadows!
Land relieved of the load of uneven yield
looks cool with the quiet moonlit meadows.
It is time to sow the seasonal seed again
Clouds cannot always cheat the potent star
Let us proceed unmindful of loss or gain
Let us plough though the bright star is afar.
We live with solid faith in our Mother Earth
Mother never deceives or wrecks her children;
It is there in our blood and veins from birth,
But who will save the Mother from this mad run.
Flocks of sheep are brought for hire to rest
for three nights to restore strength to the soil;
green manure would chase the prowling pest
Fresh plantation may yield more with our toil.
Sheep are quiet as if lulled by shepherd's song
Land is calm as a sage save the occasional bark
of our dog to chase any prowling wolf nightlong
It smiles at the moon-light from the flocking park.
Lying on the threaded cot I face the starry sky
listening to shepherd's hazards in the forest,
occasionally distracted by the nearby fox's cry;
Watching the field in the moon is delight's crest.
Nearby calls of co-farmers are like tunes of birds
that sing to cheer their mates and friendly feathers;
world slides into sleep, freed from webs of words,
Joy of moonlit peace shines beyond all weathers.
A tale of the past, a gray silver line on barren trees;
now sky-high costs drown farmers in crushing debts,
With freebies workers sit and sip the honey of bees,
Erstwhile hamlets of hard work turn into idlers' nests.

Thousand Haiku Pearls

(N.Delhi, Authors Press, 2016)

World is vast and wide
for the dynamic youth to ride
on the crest of tide.

Your sweet memories
dispel dark clouds of worries—
Light conquers night.

With smiling pearls
you make my dreary life bloom—
the spring chases gloom.

Sun and moon may rise or set
Super powers may rise and soon fall,
but crimes know no sunset.

The once famed pink city—
Royal pink exploded with terrible ink,
city bleeds and stands in dignity.

The rose, razed to the root,
her petals fondly raped and looted,
falls and faints at the foot.

Leader stands on the snowy peak,
All the snow flies with a terrible shriek
seeing his heart, a gory granite.

Cricket match—
Idle brains boundaries watch;
Reason, clean-bowled.

Management schools,
Beehives with stinging rules—

gardens of weeds.

Our Universities,
large stinking academic slums—
petty political drums.

Medical hospitals,
Leeches in golden stethoscopes—
ghosts get longer ropes.

Democracy—
a breeding ground of vices and lies
boosting dynastic rule of lice.

Buy or sell land or house—
We fill foul pockets of office;
bribe eclipses fees.

Election season
overflows with liquor and money;
goodbye to reason.

Election heat
eclipses mid-summer beat,
cools with liquor-flood.

Election promises—
countless pebbles in a near-empty pot
to pump few drops.

Freedom
exported all our black money
to Swiss banks.

Once teachers
thought of students' standards and fears,
now talk of scales and arrears.

Then teachers
referred to many reference books,
now spend in lazy looks.

Voice is a gift, a lift
To soar or sigh, use it with thrift—
a multiple choice.

Is there a weapon
more dangerous than the tongue?
a caged lion.

Tongue without a check
rides and does ruin and wreck—
a wild horse without reins

Others let us not hurt
Words have power to thrill or kill or heal
Let the thrust be on others' weal.

Words of well-wishers though harsh
are the right remedy our wrongs to thrash;
Chronic ills need bitter pills.

Trust you must
though not all, a few you trust;
oasis, a life source.

Birds fall from the sky
Lifeless on the ground they lie;
air pollution.
(5.1.2010: CNN News: in the south of US 5000
birds fell from the sky and died of a mysterious disease)
With rivers unclean,
with reckless flow of industrial effluents
life becomes lean.

Let us not pollute river water
with urban drainage and sewage flow;
life becomes shorter.

Pollution of water is a curse,
a blow to farmers and a knell to all the fish;
Life becomes worse.

Without water

wells and water bodies lose their existence;
life misses its sense.

Beauty pricks as a rose,
In its fold, wisdom many lose;
Right vision eyes miss.

Beware of beauty's power
and its wily weapon of seduction—
root of character's reduction.

Marital life
Not a bridge to burst at the seams;
To build good teams.

Man and wife are two
One they become with true love
Only to love they bow.

Man and wife
are two wheels of the same cart;
Together they fulfil life.

Wedded couple
are meant to be true friends;
Basis is trust simple.

I like her smiles
and walk with her all the miles
till the end of life.

Thought of war—
Beauty of peace it does mar
Live for right joy.

Equality is a wishful word,
At varied heights it is a flying bird;
Inequality is Nature's mark.

No two minds are equal,
No two fingers of the same hand equal;
Equality, a lip service.

Be true and respect each other,
Talk on Gender equality or inequality is a lie;
Wipe out other's tear and sigh.

Family is a huge burden;
How long to bear on these shoulders
a load heavier than boulders.

Family life—
A tumultuous sea of whirlpools,
Not a play for fools.

Rolling in dark lust
no use in breaking brains on star dust
with minds full of dust and rust.

With a rotten root
it is foolish to expect any fair fruit;
We need healthy minds.

Root out arrogance
Failure chills and kills fragrance
Will power lends dignity.

Life is a field for play
It is not a dog's fight for bones,
not a Babel of tones.

Wild animals live in caves,
Penance of sages shines in tranquil caves;
Minds sink or soar.

To reach the goal
we should play a great role;
Lead a meaningful life.

Life is a voyage vague
with piercing cries of human bombs;
Terrorist, a plague.

Corporate hospitals

money-minting unethical machines—
Trading portals.

Most medical doctors
are commission agents and cunning actors;
amassing money, their only creed.

Ninety out of a hundred
these physicians loot and live on brokerage
in a graded stage.

From pills to scans and rays
all tests to final rest are minting ways—
Monsters in medical life.

Corruption is the cancer
It incarnates in multiple forms
Uproot it with a lancer.

We specialize the art
of making the simple into complex
to realize our part.

Brainless fools bet
with toiled drops of sweat;
Players roll in millions.

Cinemas are a bane,
packed with dirty sex and violence;
Morals on the wane.

Human bombs a menace
From cold massacre terrorists don't rest;
An epic contest.

Terrorists are a horrible threat
to humanity and human civilization;
Apply pesticide to kill the pest.

A leader to be a tree
that receives all the heat and spreads shade;

Service is not a trade.

Religion is a footboard
to reach the divine feet of the Lord
in any form on any road.

Earthly glories go away
with all the glow and glitter and sway
with the touch of the Icy Hand.

Mark of our civilization—
Passion and pleasure, the modern way,
Fashion of the day.

Mammon's power game—
We dance to the tunes of wealth
and amass by stealth.

Now money rules,
In fact it is the measuring rod;
All else is a clod.

Castes and creeds
are man-made walls; demolish them
and uproot the weeds.

Our goal is not in sight,
Let us fight for our natural right;
Life is a struggle.

Need of the hour
is to straighten the curves of destiny
Great is will power.

To get a true friend
is like finding water in a desert;
Life may end.

Dharma is eternal,
Living beings now or later perish;
Moral values cherish.

Truths don't change
We may drink water in a mirage;
Fools we can't enlighten.

Wedded couple
to rest on the rock bed of love and trust;
Truth is a must.

There is a price tag,
Morals and values in market we sell;
Life is in pell-mell.

Strive for peace;
War is death and horrible havoc,
Mutual wreck.

Putting a wreath
on a known or unknown corpse—
Politician's wealth.

In thought be tall
Break down Berlin walls and Chinese walls
Enter wider hall.

Open thy mind's gate,
in receiving higher thoughts don't be late;
Let noble thoughts flow.

Beasts we can't tame;
Vicious act of killing or kidnap—
A cold-blooded game.

From the ashes of the past
rise fires of the present and future—
a thoughtful venture.

Inner echo spreads
though temple bells cease to ring
with a higher wing.

In all see the divine—
Bird or beast, fly or reptile, man or swine;

Behind the breath is He.

I search for my guide,
He exists unseen in the world wide;
I stand perplexed.

These mortal ears
are His Grace to listen to His glory;
It chases all fears.

God's thought never rings
when our hearts are bound by strings
of bonds and carnal lust.

Search of soul
though it is late, let us start;
a conscious chart.

Unless we cross
this delusion and material dross
we can't see the light.

To realize the Self
as long as this mind does ramble
it is a mere gamble.

Let us be willing tools
in the hands of God to do His work;
We can no more be fools.

With prayer unsaid
let us not think of going to bed;
Confession is good.

Aspire for lasting glow;
For material gains don't stoop low—
fading bubbles.

Life on earth is an iron gate;
Beyond the dark iron gate and the golden gate
shines the true Light of lights.

This life is a golden chance,
Know Him and enjoy His grace and glance;
Time spent is time lost.

Make a beginning,
Not to try to know Him is a curse;
Life turns worse.

If we ignore the Lord
life becomes a wild cry of rage;
a useless page.

Devotion to God
leads us to His abode on celestial track,
to earth never to be back.

Thanks to Mother Nature
the kinetic power of the Lord
the only ruling God.

High above the Lord reigns,
He is beyond our eyes and brains;
Devotion is the only way.

The eternal Director
is beyond the bounds of Time and Space;
Only Truth can see His face.

God is omnipresent,
Let us seek with one mind and heart;
He will never part.

Our minds will sink,
He is beyond the range of ink and think;
Surrender is the only way.

Morals matter most,
Noble thoughts let us cherish
Or soon we perish.

Desires are huge waves;
them at their birth let us arrest

or we lose peace and rest.

Devotion is fragrance
Grasp and clasp of spirit to be the mark
Prayer a minute arc.

Meditation is the path
Useless is all this shallow talk
Long is the walk.

Let us know the Self
with will and hope more and more;
we will reach the shore.

To reach the divine
path is razor-sharp, hard and long;
primordial sound and song.

Inside shines the spark,
This physical body is a house of clay;
Sensual desires let us slay.

Let the mind rest on Him;
Life is the same old tedious story
if it fails to sing His glory.

Supreme is the Lord;
The day His glory is not sung
is a curse to the tongue.

Lord leaves us free
We are free to shine or burn in furnace
He is the pure Witness.

Lord shines in act and art,
resides hidden in the cave of the heart;
Being and Non-Being is He.

Light is Knowledge;
These useless bulbs why do we store?
True light restore.

Acquire higher knowledge,
Like fire it burns whatever is dark;
Light is the only mark.

The chanting of Ohm
spreads vibrations of sublime charm;
Mind becomes calm.

Beyond the visible sphere
The Self is pure as stainless glass;
One-minded let us pass.

Lord is One and only One,
Above the stars the Supreme Star;
For devotees there is no bar.

It is the Infinite Light,
The Supreme has neither form nor name,
the All-lighting flame.

We are impure;
with this heavy baggage, the sinful load
We can't cross the road.

The One Supreme
is beyond the limits of form and norm;
Let us be calm.

To realize a piece of the Self
before this body becomes old and cold;
the Spirit must be bold.

Un-published Poems

Our Race

What is wrong with our race?
We stand always last in the race
We always limp and are lost in the blast
Right from childhood cells of my mind are trained
and tuned to the strains of fear and slavery;
righteous rage and courage are alien things
We always blink, sink and shrink to think
of our once cherished concept 'Be fearless'
and prefer to live in the heinous hell of fear
and in the shell of cheerless solitude.
We relish to propagate this attitude
We feel proud of our seeming democracy
which is a cute count in mute numbers.
For over a thousand years all these staggering numbers
failed to make us bold, made us dumb and numb;
while numbers fail a few members rule --
the ruthless rule and roast, reign and whine.
We suffer from old haunting memories,
marooned memories of horrible histories
of butchers, breakers and massacred millions,
sickening pages red with streams of blood
that turned our stream of conscience red;
then we were fleeced by the alien wolves,
now by the ruthless cruel native wolves.
There is nothing to feel proud of our past,
our history, past and present, is flooded
with ceaseless blunders and ruthless plunders;
a faint ray of hope for this timid race lies
in the lightening words of our ancient sages
whose message shines through ageless ages
which can stir and spur and recharge the race,
in the clouded sky a thin line of silvern lace.

Let us Rise

How can you hurl me into dust?
Never can you do it, me you can't bind;
I'll rise from dust like a whirlwind,
Like the morning sun or evening star
I will rise dispelling the hostile cloud
Like the defiant tide I shall defy thy move
and strongly stage a robust come-back.
Envy makes you break down
in fact I pity your sullen state
till you change unawares to a cloud;
I shall not bow down though you cause my fall
Neither your words nor your looks
can unnerve me, can kill or chill me;
from the ire and fire of your eyes
I am sure to rise like a livid flame
that makes you lame and tame,
lose the balance and lick the dust;
From the greyish clouds of envy and neglect
I shall rise till my word swells like a tide
that rides through the world;
word is my gift, truly God's gift,
my fallen people it is sure to lift;
I refuse to be your bonded slave,
I'll rise and raise my fallen brethren
with my wounded word, still brave;
To all the drunken bulls that try to dominate
with a firm hand let me put a checkmate.
Today's corrupt political scene raises its ugly head
with tomorrow's haunting treacherous history;
Let me dispel the cloud of hysteria with my pen
sharp as razor and potent as an atomic tool,
with my word to clean this piled up dust.

A Caged Bird

I wish to fly and sing like a koel
here I am a caged bird
feet are tied, wings flap in vain
I am tired to the core, throat gets choked
fails to sing with natural ease;
with hands tied and heart in strings

whom should I please in this short span;
I am a slave in my own house,
a greater slave in my village;
when the word of the politician is law
every move is a move in bondage
every word, designed to please
every act is stage-managed.
How can a slave sing in the field
though the canopy above is unbounded?
Voice emerges deep from the well,
but it is dull, free from thrill,
sounds hoarse and hollow by the hill;
Freedom makes life full and rich
Feeling free my song will touch the skies,
liberated my tune floats and flows,
kisses leaves and petals that dance
in woods, groves and wider fields
and touches strings of heart within.

Savage Space

In this infinite universe
beyond the reach of human mind
this is a tiny planet where we live
and wander through savage space
facing the hostile heat of the sun
without ever reaching the destination
without ever trying to know the truth
eternal and startling, but not sensational
which needs a brave and single heart
that firmly believes in peace and serene ways
to greet people with a joyous hand
not to raise hostile hands and clenched fists
or to try to hold the sun in your palm
Before the colourful curtain falls
though any day certain it is to fall
let us revive and resuscitate the land
bruised and battered beyond recognition
where the grass is stained with blood
reactivate the benumbed fallen faces
sunken and drunken, sore and swollen,
with torn out bodies and scattered mass of flesh;
while banners of countries and continents tremble

in tornadoes of atomic dust and deluge
and perfect scanners shiver and sink in dread
while rackets reign in schools and temples
rituals are performed with the incense
of hollow impious breath and foul money;
where flags are hoisted on the burning bodies
of deafening landmines in the name of change
of a wider range of death and destination
when can we see the change to a golden face?
Though the winter night is freezingly long
none can arrest the arrival of the twilight
or the beaming rays chasing the shadows;
children will surely smile as flowers bloom
and koels won't fail to greet with their tunes.

Dignity in Exile

Let us confess that Great Walls and Pyramids
Towers and Taj structures that stand as giants
are in fact not great wonders of ancient peace
or prosperity, people's dignity, glory or grace;
Built with whips and cudgels and spears
on pools of sweat, tears, blood and broken bones
on the bonded labour and collapsed bodies
of thousands of unlettered slavish sub-humans
they stand now in veiled gory glory;
We feel proud of these wonders
that stand on the glittering glassy pages
Our existence is an hourly struggle, a challenge
in the midst of all-consuming exploitation
cut-throat competition and speeding death
lurking and waiting in multiple forms and ways.
AS long as we feel content with rituals and gestures
as our school children carry lifeless flags
in the polluted lanes sweating in the sun
and our greedy leaders hoist helpless flags
as a matter of vanity food for media,
as long as our temple priests and officers
give special harathi to new-hatched chicks
in golden fields, tinsel stars and cricket stars
and these idle priests worship matinee idols,
true dignity cannot set its foot on this land

and there will not be place for true values;
solemnity sinks and cleanliness goes in exile.
Only when average hands reveal their tender touch
with their kind and truly healing aura
we can boldly cross the threatening gulfs of chaos
and devouring divisions dark and devilish,
commotions and contradictions and convergences
and make this tolerable for the average man;
these are not the days of oracles and miracles,
let all the miracles and wonders of the world
revolve round the axis of 'Live and let live'.
Or we will miss the rapture of the rainbow
and the blinding brilliance of the lightning,
the thrilling splendour of the Niagara Falls,
the enchanting beauty of the Luray Caves,
the rejuvenating unearthly eternal aura
of the gushing waters of the sacred Ganga.

Smiling Riddle

Can we feel the pulse of man
or the pulse of the cooing morn
or the pulse of the cooling moon
in the vibrating lines of a verse;
the gloom and the gloomy moon give way
to the crowing dawn and the cawing morn
the rays, the silent alarming bells
of the marching sun announce
the hot arrival with a warm welcome;
Can anyone draw this thrill of changing shades
growing richer and richer every moment
mixing mangoes, apples and cherries
from the lunar cleaving of eastern hills,
poet or painter in lines or lined verse
that can capture the rising golden glory?
One gives the faint spark of the early phase,
the other catches the light of the later rays,
while the mighty middle heaves and leaves a riddle
that smiles at the little brush and the poor pen
baffling the two from the higher realm.

Media the Medusa

What is there to write
no day passes without a risk;
what is there to speak
where corruption is at its peak;
what is there to read
when almost all of us do bleed,
when media is fond of mass masala
spreading wild rumours, cancer tumours
and newspapers become private pamphlets;
Morning news paper spreads foul smell
of rotten tomatoes rising in its pitch
as the sickening smell of a rotten rat
by the wide roadside with traffic jam
 wet with stagnant drops of stingy rain.
All these papers are like thrown away leaves
at the end of a corrupt political banquet,
spicy smell soon spreading the foul odour
hitting the nose and spreading the noose,
full of lifeless puns and guns scoring zero runs
stuffed with sensational lies, not a slice of truth;
Truth is scared of our sight, human sight,
We don't like to care for cleanliness,
mind to be clean, tongue to be clean;
Morally we are nil or lean sans any sheen.

Beneath the Colour

Colour of the skin shines
as a burning topic for the thin;
Butcher's blade knows
beneath the skin, thick or thin,
blood is red, apple red;
though skin is white or black
milk is white, cotton white;
crow and crane wing the sky
and perch on the same bough.
We start like different streams
from different hills and peaks
but end in the same sea.
One shows the head,
the other glows with tail,

both the head and the tail
refer to the same old tale.

Million March

Million hands rise with clenched fists
the echo of their cries rends cold mists
and centuries of servile dark ignorance;
The day is tediously long, hot and dry
armed chairs and crowns deaf to the cry
centuries of encrusted darkness is thick
The widened wound is big and sick
Million gasping cries of bruised breath
boldly face and resist armed iron hands.
Our untidy hands are tied, lips are sealed,
why need a dip in the helpless Ganges?
Dogs and guns bark in wide ranges
Night is eerily cold and fiercely long;
All who raise their voice and throng
are pushed to the cruel Chinese wall
that relishes to arrest and crush their call;
While wicked guns wildly bang and bark
sound explodes the clouded sky in the dark.
Walls of rock are stony strong and high
and blindly prevent sweet fruits to reap.
Let us open our eyes and on firm foot rise,
Though history is red with pages of pain
let us strive and struggle to be free again
and open the valves of our reluctant hearts
and find unity in all the divided parts.
The noble minds of the million march
for nobler thoughts, a huge greeting arch.
Fanatics and fundamentalists in mad frenzy
rave, rant and kill fundamentals of ethics
Desert voices of crushed democratic minds
lie endangered in the whirlpool of sandstorm,
but springs of oases with pleasant winds
are sure to revive life in a nobler form.

Kinship

Yes, he says he is my kin
but the bond, a hair line, is so thin,

though from the same old branch;
Showers of rain wet the garden
seeds sprout, grow rich and branch,
a few blossom fast with fairer fruits
while a few derange minds to the roots
 Dark clouds the azure sky embrace
to darken the earth beyond trace
The meaning of traditional kin
does not go beyond the skin
with age it has grown so pale and thin;
Red organic links are danger signs
says our precise modern science;
Let us stand aloof from the veil
to escape the day to wait and wail,
try to tear the veil and see the light
beyond the tunnel even at night;
Garden blooms with children's smiles
and shines with glowing fireflies.

Enigma

Hair has turned white as cotton
passing through all the milestones of years
nearing the last one still devoid of cheers;
all the gloried aims are blown and beaten
with mocking beads of blasted bubbles
and pricking thorns of ceaseless troubles;
with all our drilled and grilled actions
we fail to see the light even in fractions;
Right is wrong and wrong is right
for the rich with power and might;
All our acts seem mere trivial things,
patches of airy puff in fading rings;
All the acts and facts we feel central,
these gloried days and deeds we feel eternal
are indeed baubles and bubbles ephemeral.

The Beaten Track

Let me not tread the defaced trodden path
though a walk ago for many the chosen way
Overnight people turned on it their wrath
Possible, familiarity breeds quick contempt.

Not all have prohibited it as squarely wrong
for reasons best known to them as strong;
    a few still cling to it and sing, a few shrink
they know the old is gold, yet they limp and blink.
Their dark deeds have danced in a trance,
clouds overpower and envelope the day,
Day with mutilated wings lies a fallen prey,
Negative powers grow strong in dark, they say.
The bold and the old alike like the golden track
Though a beaten track, they don't go back.
Men, brave and grave, shrink to fight the stink,
Shut their ears and go back to sleep and sink;
While lame legs run, blind eyes glow as fireflies
Where power corrupts, fear buries the truth.
Father, Father, glowing bright high above,
hide not your luminous face behind the rainbow;
Uproot the vicious wild weed with lightning speed
and with thy thunder protect those that bleed.

Don't Write Me Off

Don't write me off as dead
I am not dead, but I am dead-tired
Resurrected I will rise instead;
the same old talk, the same old walk,
no life in talk, no life in walk or chalk;
Colours get diluted with dry tears,
sketch too dim, tainted and faded,
a confusing mass of paradoxical mask
a vague mirror of this pitiable plight;
No leaf, nor flower, only dry bark,
Out of lifeless seed sprouts the new breed;
I am the seen and the seer without seeing
Beyond the eyes is the invisible scene
Where should I rest, when there is no ideal nest?
Yes I can wait for the call for a quiet rest;
I prefer to miss the glitter of this scene
to the distant hope of the seer's grace.

Novel Bonds

Unknown bonds covertly enter
All on a sudden spouse descends

from the starry sky as a better half,
then sons and daughters tumble
from nowhere in this infinite cosmos
and encroach into still vacant space;
Soon their spouses drop from vacuum
enter from unknown quarters
to live and love, share and reign;
Old bonds fade as new links arrive
from unexplored areas with greater drive
like blinding lightnings from the dark sky;
old waters give way to fresh waters
with the downpour of seasonal rains;
these bonds make us bonded slaves,
childish fools and arrant knaves
missing and forgetting the right path,
and pursue gold and glitter with envious greed,
things, vanishing creams and passing dreams;
All these multiple onerous knotted bonds
thrive and strengthen with growing age
make us live as croaking frogs in ponds;
these bonds force us to work like bulls
till we gasp for breath and collapse;
Unawares we are freed from these ties
with this sudden exit from the noisy stage.

Invisible Manes

We are the blasted scattered spirits
untimely cut unawares ere we bloomed
buds without shield or yield half ripe
for no fault of ours, innocent souls;
No enmity, nor vengeance, nor hate,
We are reconciled to our tragic fate;
Those that killed us knew not our faces
nor we theirs, poor unknown hirelings.
Haters of creed, breed and land's sacred seed
on the other side of the border richly relish
to drink our blood to their stomach's fill,
our scattered flesh and limbs their fiendish dish.
Now ours is a force to reckon with
a formidable band of potent invisible manes
fiery salamanders burning with revenge
waiting for the nod of the land's passive head

not a thinking one, but a timid and an erratic one,
a dynastic head without one on the shoulders
making a mockery of the democratic state;
He wants to build his empire on our red remnants
an empire of umpires watching over burning pyres.
We strongly wish to resurrect our consumed forms
and save this land and her children from burning fires.
Before we are forgotten and our memories wiped out
we want to invite you for our party of blasted bodies
to taste the varied stuff of our dismembered limbs
in the midst of drunken revelry and licensed liquor
on which our state's sinking economy survives
which our corrupt leaders relish with eyes blind
to the extended geography of terror and hunger.

To quit or not to quit?

To quit or not to quit right now
is the rocking problem;
The clouded situation of the now
and the broken view of this old overused nest
deprives me of quiet rest
 Aged wings refuse to fly
tired feet to march feel shy
These brittle bones, partly broken,
a temple on the verge of collapse,
hurl a vain challenge, but significant
while the multiple lines on the brow
delve deep into the aged rings
hardened with dents and defeats;
but no regrets, only truce;
if I live, I live to learn and stay
like a dew drop on the lotus leaf
and try to the end to know.
Without dwelling on the end
let me reflect on my gracious Father
and all the time on Him let me spend.

The Graph of our Acts

No use in pinpointing the old cracks
no use in running on parallel tracks
to the treacherous walls of carnal lures;

With will let us turn our bandaged backs,
the magic of will power let us not lose or lack;
Real facts are sure to draw the graph of our acts,
Let folks and neighbours loudly laugh at us,
soon at leisure we too can laugh at them;
only patience, not wealth or power, we need,
the only balm the miracle when we bleed.
I may not cosily lie or stand on top
I know I am not a feeble fallen drop;
my life may not be a seventh heaven,
how can it be without the better half
whom the Almighty snatched away;
but it is a fact it is not a hell;
The departed soul strengthens the departing soul;
The thought of the love of the dear departed
is a big transformer, energizer and Vitamin B,
it urges me to stand erect on my old legs,
never to be a parasite or an idle walker,
but with the firm luminous self to shine;
my act of planting sees me rise beyond the planet.
Memories of golden moments are fresh and green.
Unbidden they beckon me to visit the gloried past,
Not a borrowed fleeting flash of a carnal kiss
but the realized dream of a shared bliss,
treasured till the end, unfaded and unfading.

15th August

As usual it is 15th August!
Innocent students with flaming hearts assemble
and stand in front of the blinking flag;
Flags are flatly hoisted by our fat leaders,
strangers to the semantic spirit of the word;
from raised pedestal they struggle to speak
with inflated bellies and deflated brains
on the poor pure departed selfless souls,
once a well-known mighty patriotic gallery,
who laid down their lives and all they had.
Enthroned high on their engraved graves
jackals devour and belch in democratic garb,
borrow the technique from their superiors
and apply cunningly to grind the hungry axes
by fleecing the stupid and selfish flocks.

Children get chocolates for standing in the sun
while masses loads of liberal promises.
Burning cause for freedom struggle lies
safely buried afar in the forgotten graves;
their long departed souls are shell-shocked
to see their seeds of supreme sacrifice with roots
grown too heavy with black poisoned fruits;
they blink, shiver in sheer dread and weep,
and pray the Lord to save the land ere they sleep.

Let None Share my Tears

These blooms are mine, these blames are mine
These fears are mine, these tears are mine
Let me share my radiant smiles with you
Let me carry these piercing tears with me
Waves of joy in others' faces give me joy
Rays of sunny smiles on others make me shine
'Fair is foul, foul is fair', the great sage said,
I don't have wits or guts to say so,
but I own both the fair and the foul
though I hate the sight of the owl;
its eyes and face shoot volleys of fear,
its frightening cry I shudder to hear;
Let me wipe the tears on others' eyes,
Let my words free them from gloomy sighs,
while springs of my heart sustain their smiles,
while strings of my heart shall hold my pains;
Let none share my tears, I bear my tears to my pyre
with the last smile twinkling at my last fading fire.

The Veil

A veil on one's face, eyes and heart
When we fail we want to veil
Not to fail we veil, Veil wails to veil
We are afraid of truth, we are afraid of light;
Can I hide myself, my self
Shades are many and murky
We can't bask behind the mask
Let me blast this maverick mask
I know it is an uphill task
How long should I hide behind the veil,

How long can we play hide and seek?
With this veil we can't sail
With this vicious veil
to the shore can we sail ?
Can we see the Supreme Light
the light of the face of God
hidden behind Nature's veil,
the invisible maya, the Golden Veil?

Space

In this sphere there is ample space
in every field for wild and corrupt race
for the changing shades of human face,
more often with a morbid menace;
but little space for frightened peace
in this vast globe amid hot and cold wars
and ruthless blood-thirsty acts of terrorism,
the monstrous face of mindless fanaticism;
more space for sham, hate and shame,
little space for truth, ethics and fame;
more space for travesty, little space for honesty;
more space for might, little space for the right;
more space for wine, dine and dance,
grab and swallow or vomit in tipsy trance;
little space for clean and pure fragrance;
Save some scanty space for the righteous
and the vanishing tribe of the nobly brave
and for the famished grace in the grave.

Let us Wait

What is this life? A crux, a riddle?
A clueless question, a baffling quest!
No rest, always a pest till it goes to dust.
This life is a vast polluted playground
Willy-nilly we have to play the game
till we complete our ordained round
whether we reap in turn fame or shame;
It is a stream that runs riotous and rough,
often clear on sandy stretch or on slimy slough;
Wait till a living statue springs from a hard rock
till the breathless stroke of a chisel on a stone block;

Let us wait with a wick in the hoping eye
to see rubies in cheeks, not a tear or a sigh;
With a firm resolve to seek and strive,
to be brave and proactive and not to bow.
Facing the clear clouded sunny sky
let us catch the elusive thrill of the rainbow.
With wounded wing we can't soar heavenward
Let us drag the life as it flows and wait till it glows;
Let us wait, there is time for everything
The moment we plant a seed we can't get the fruit.

Frog's Leap

Birth a comma, a big question mark
the yield of an animal spark;
childhood a stupid helpless stage,
youth a burning volcanic page,
old age a package of regrets with spells of sleep;
end an abrupt full stop,
life a sketch of frog's leap -
an exclamation, a short paragraph
too brief for a lucid monograph.
Betwixt comma and stop many causes
full of credits and debits with clauses,
unchartered zones and unwanted acts,
unexplored tracts and inexplicable facts;
Alas! Borders bulge and grudge,
more often blink and sink and stink,
tear the slough of sleep not so deep
and come out to bask in the sun in a leap.

Regain the Vision

How can I explain your mind, a sealed cover
I am not a clairvoyant or a magician with power;
I know I'm bit of a mental man against the wind,
Sometimes I can read the periphery of your mind
and can draw external diagrams, an outline sketch;
with all antics and oddities, I am a tolerable wretch;
of course I can draw a linear graph on the rise and fall
of your unpredictable moods and demands tall;
In fact I am pennywise and pound foolish;
How can I know your hidden holistic self

when in fact I fail to understand my own self?
This creation is at once a chaos and confusion
a constant riddle and an enigmatic rhythm;
We are experts in browsing the internet
but zeroes in seeing our minds' internet;
We connect ourselves to the notion of a nation
but we fail to have a fixed destination,
though the final one is inevitable to all;
Wherever we land on heights in flights
land we must in dust in clueless nights.
All these hates and spates of hits and wits fade
and vanish in black hole before the dark shade.
It is a pity while birds flap in joy, we flop;
they live in truth on truth with nature
while we roll and romp in false identification
with deceptive glitters, litters and jitters
with all shades of ego, logo, tear, fear and hate
and flee far away from the path of truth
depending on kith and kin, huge leviathans,
that relish outspoken barbs and bullets
and unspoken murderous thoughts and acts;
they shine with hind sight and sixth sense
which we totally lack with our blurred vision;
Our past cultures stand as blind lampposts,
mute spectators and deflated check-posts;
unless we go back to our long forgotten path
of sanatana dharma re can't regain the light
to see things in proper light with vision right.

Down the Memory Lane

I stand stranded on the chaotic road
flanked by tall buildings as soldiers bold
submerged in clouds of emission of smoke
and pollution at a high pitch at every stroke;
eyes become blurred with columns of dust,
now not medical but ethical cure is a must;
mind becomes crazy with varied wild tones,
drops of grief percolate from other zones
as fragile as our rickety fingerprints
defaced by hurt and dirt, harm and charm;
This tear with all your skill you can't capture
it leads to a blurring bleeding fracture;

We may not relish it down the memory lane
often we need bitter pills to keep us sane;
The end may bring a little shade of peace
but earth's space is too vast for human pace.

Prime Source and Seed

One and only One multiplies in millions,
Without name or form He shines in all names
and forms, living and non-living,
that converge at last and unite in the One;
No loss, no gain; whole is whole;
divided or deducted, It remains the same;
The only norm, He is above all norms,
All little lamps and candles merge in wider light,
All the suns, stars, and moons draw their light
from the prime shining Source and Seed.
When It shines, then all else shines;
when It lights, all else lights and glows;
Beyond the light and endless night
forever It blazes, the Eternal Light.

Learn from Birds

In front of the aesthetic western house
two lush green bushes with care grow
Beneath the bushy plants moves a mouse
basks in the warm sun and runs slow.
A hundred sparrows flow from the bush
from webs of leaves and tiny boughs
that arrest the sunny rays and rainy rush
Even to freezing snow it never bows.
A hundred birds in a single bush rest
They fly and merrily play around the plant
Soon they come under the wings of the nest
They fly and sing in joy free from want.
One bush thick and green, ten feet high
Grows like a globe, two metres wide
The other, like a pyramid, grows neck-high
 To multitudes of birds shelter they provide.
While bigger trees happily host larger birds
Smaller ones in smiles shelter tender wings
But man's endless wants are beyond words

To all the land and reeking riches he clings.

Mouse and Mountain

One evening a little mouse near the fountain
under the peepal tree spoke to the big mountain:

Though I am small in size, I am big in little life
From your foot I tread to your head and peaks
I dig and cut your deeps with my teeth as a knife
I scan your riches and ditches, lows and leaks.

All living entities from ants, flies, bugs and bees
to deers, tigers and elephants walk on your chest
birds and monkeys fly and play on your green trees
Snakes and reptiles loot and on thy chest they rest.

Of all this wild havoc and plunder you are the victim
Though you are of mud and stone you rest as a rock
With all our cruel mischief, we are slim and trim
Are you too weak to punish and give them a shock?

Mountain in high majesty gave the classic reply:
They are all too little and tiny things for me to think
They all come and go, rise, roar and fly, fall and cry
Poor creatures! Let empty bubbles blink and sink.

Glow Worm

Twinkle, twinkle firefly, pretty glow worm!
Field and grassy ground become fairly warm
Are they little stars or tempting serial lights
They grab our hearts and illumine dewy nights.

They may not scale the realm of higher sky
But they form another starry sky as they fly
So humble, they do not look at the far off star
The fall of the tiny wings does its glory mar.

As we look at the field, you charm our hearts
To paint thy charm is beyond the bounds of arts
Thy winning spree flies with a surer stellar start
With or without wings none can play your part.

On blades of grass you turn and twist, glide and glow
You dance and play hide and seek as winds blow.
Are they little stars or has the sky come down
to illumine the night and bless this tiny town?

A Song to Sing

This is the song, my brethren, we need to sing
till in our distracted minds unity it does ring.

There alone atop the snowy Himalayan hill
our betrayed Mother with flooded swollen eyes
weeps that turns even the turbulent winds still
and flying wings stand still for a while in the skies.

We her children with minds corrupt to the core
with evil designs and greed for wealth and power
now spread the creed of hate with peace no more
fighting with bombs of foulest words every hour.

A few satanic tongues vitiate the pleasant climate
They are hell-bent sooner to spread the wild fires
and reach their wily goal and rule the bleeding state
by bisecting and sucking Mother's blood as vampires.

We cursed the alien rule and scheme of divide and rule
though their rule developed and united us at last;
This vast land these evil brains manage to fool
Souls of freedom fighters cry to see this unity lost.

With an upright head chase the dark divisive forces
Let each drop of our blood echo the spirit of unity
With clean minds advance with our rich resources
Make our Mother Bharat smile with unity in diversity.

This is the song, my brethren, we need to sing
till in our misguided minds unity it does ring.

Can Wounded Wing Sing?

Can a bird fly with a wounded wing,
In wringing pain can it sing?

Melodic note becomes dumb.
Can peacock dance in delight
with its full range of feathers
when the cruel tiger is at sight?
Can a dog stop its barking in a louder plane
where another one comes from the next lane
to snatch by force its fleshy bone?
Can a bruised horse run in a gallop
when its bleeding legs fail to move and hop
when the distressed body falls as a drop?
Can a hungry human heart
smile without a tinge of borrowed art
and pray the Lord with a whole heart?
Can the moon shine in full light
when it is in total eclipse at night
and loses all the milky shine?
Can the strings of mother's heart throb
when she hears the child's sob
or when the child is snatched away?
Let us bow to mother's love!
Freedom and joy lead to peace.

A Strange World

What is this world full of cares and snares,
How long should I wait and watch?
No time to eat or drink beneath the roof
We are busy as bees and we need proof;
No time to sit and talk under the greenwood tree
From dawn to dusk we work, we are not free;
No time to recharge our minds in the forest
Birds and animals do, but we have no rest;
No time to feel the fragrance of flowers or relish its beauty
Even at night, we receive calls of duty;
No time to look at the moon and stars in the sky
Our life has become a vast desert dreary and dry;
No time to listen to the sacred words of sages
Life is drowned in earning and burning wages;
No time to think of the Creator and pray
To clubs and pubs and screens we have fallen a prey;
No time to listen to koel's music or sound of sparrow
Of greed and lust we are struck by aching arrows.
This is a strange world of glow and gloomy patch

No longer can we wait in queue and watch.

Shed not a Tear (A Sonnet)

Do not weep or shed any tear, my child
When I die, it is only a brief pause and a welcome change
World's ways are wild, you are still mild
change we must, system or body – a wide range
When I die, die we must, do not weep at my grave
Discard we should our old and worn out dress
Never do we regret, we put on a new one with a brave face
Our friends, all and sundry, donning it we impress.
 We are the dazzling rays of the burning sun
who draws the light from the Supreme Light
We are the blades of grass and drops of rain that run
We enter only to leave; so child, be bold and bright.
We are the atoms of that deathless Super Soul
(Ants and mountains, seas and stars, plants and planets)
All exist through That and are parts of that One Whole.

Seeking Peace

Beyond form is the storm in the heart
At times for no reason I feel as a windy leaf shaky
From cool and tranquil mind I migrate and part
Even in alien shores my will is still crystal rocky.

Amid the rocky fort I still feel solidly insecure
Surrounding envy in the rural past and present
Though uncertain as a bubble is this tenuous tenure
It has probably moulded me to be a little reticent.

I like to be simple and always unassuming
That is why I failed to harvest the right opportunities
By nature I am averse to feigning devious veiling
and ostentatious ways, trivialities and vanities.

Unable to dismantle the cobwebs of old structures
We prefer to live in our snug self-knit gossamer nest
Diffident to embark on innovative ventures
We train our minds to feel cosy in muddled rest.

Contrary winds threaten to dislodge and dissolve

Forces in and out distract and hurl me in confusion
Against the vicious tide I sail with a firm resolve
Before Time runs out let me gain in inner vision.

Let me strive to seek peace and the latent light
and see the inner Lord boundless and golden bright.

Snakes and Ladders

After thirty years of service I still stagnate,
Most of my colleagues pity at my fate;
Where I once began I would at last end,
We accept this vote bank political trend;
Juniors to my juniors are now my big bosses,
Where should I wail for decades of my losses?
They look down upon me from the top,
Like frogs from step to higher step they hop.
While for decades I rot at the rung in life sadder,
they find themselves by leaps atop the ladder;
The system, blindfolded, mocks at my state and says:
You are born high, always work and rot low,
To hell with your service and merit till date!
The lower the caste, the higher and faster you grow.
May I appeal to the Lord to reserve a berth
in the most favoured caste in my next birth!
He may laugh; in all He is; we are His trace,
In His eyes there is no high or low caste or race.
This caste by birth is a sinful sequel of a devil's mind
cemented by heinous selfish forces blind;
Can we remove one word by another word,
Can we crush a rotten seed by sowing a foul seed?
Remove the stink of the division of cruel caste
by true education, developing the state and taste;
For the ancient sin we are forced to pay the price;
We are deprived; we lose, we fall; Can we rise?
Let us bury this caste ten thousand fathoms deep,
Let not the cancer of caste make our lives weep,
Let us tread the bright path of Sanatana Dharma
and feel the glory of sunrise by severing caste karma.
Caste as a cobra bites some; for some it is a ladder;
Should we play this vicious game of snakes and ladders?

Lines on a Dog

Since a fortnight it stayed at the grave
the grave of his master young and kind
in sun and shower its heart is firm and brave
Its breathed his last in an accident blind

His kith and kin left after his burial there
His faithful dog his pet for five long years
cried and cried; the loss it could not bear
It scratched the grave with eyes full of tears.

And waited to see the master resurrect and rise;
Members of Blue Cross Society saw this
It heeded not their calls and gestures to be wise
In waiting and starving at the grave it found its bliss.

Facts they found and brought the youth's mother
She saw the missing dog, thought it had left
Amid grief and rituals, about it she didn't bother
When she saw it there her heart in twain was cleft.

The dog, lean and sad, kissed her feet with moist eyes
Her eyes welled with tears, took it in her arms
Soon with the dog she left the place full of sighs
The dog dumb and loyal stood for eternal norms.

Note:- This poem is based on a real incident at Avadi burial ground, Chennai. Soon after, the mother left the place and went with the dog to Tiruvannamalai. Source: *The Times of India* (Internet News) Sept. 2014

When I Pass Away

The day when I pass away
with feet uprooted from this clay
flying to some undiscovered land
channelled by the great invisible hand.
Let me fade as a fleece of cloud
let me recede as morning fog
let me vanish as a whirling puff of smoke
let me fade as an autumnal fallen leaf
without a tear from a dear eye
free from the heat of a heavy sigh

and slightest gesture of grief;
With a face fresh as morning leaf
let the heart bid adieu with a smile
that can recharge to wing countless miles
miles and miles in space to sing God's glory.

Death Blues

Death is a cause, a clause
Death is a result, a pause,
a pass for peace, a break,
a break from neck-break;
Pushed with the back to the wall
like a hunted hog, I won't fall
I will face with head erect and brave
and fight the dark evil forces
till I enter the certain grave.
After the exit of the spark
why should I care for this body?
Whether I am burnt or buried
ashes are kept in an urn
or thrown into the sea or sky
or in the waters of the Ganges,
it is immaterial for me;
what matters is - how I live, not how I die.

Fall Foliage

Summer's warming days lose their edge
hostile rays miss their prime punch and power
Slyly ushers fall with cool breeze as a bridge
Fall tolls the end of frowning heat with windy shower
Smiles of lilies, daffodils, tulips and roses steadily fade
Their proud petals, tired of their dance, pale and fall;
Till now a mighty colourful army, recedes in shade,
Their residual numbers timidly fail to enthral.
Trees invite fleecy clouds with their countless leaves
Soon leaves lustrous transform to fairer flowers
while their sickly sisters faint and fall as untied sheaves;
These legion leafy flowers vie with the stellar stars
If stars yonder in the sky proudly twinkle at night
these charming leaves shine in day with equal right;
Day to day progress of the charm of changing colours

feasts the eye and robs the hearts of nature lovers;
These colour changes are beyond the painter's brush
Their spell arrests the eyes with celestial bridal blush
Their changing hues shine and steal our enthralled hearts
The charm of alchemic change is above the power of arts;
Green to greenish dark, overnight it turns to light rose,
then to princely pink and incarnates in pretty purple pose;
Woods and forests cease to be weary, weirdly and wooden,
appear as an enchanting fairy land rosy and golden;
Maple leaves change to rosy glow, then to apple red,
gliding from shade to shade, cherry-red, dapple-bred;
Leaves of some stay turmeric yellow as wise sages,
Season-sick soon they fade and fall with age in stages;
Chameleon's change of colours is defensive and repulsive,
colour change of leaves is a luxuriant leafy fest attractive;
Niagara falls in all seasons is an awesome splendour
These fall colours in chosen lands create a rare wonder
Taj, a marble beauty, bores with its only stone in white
Treasure of fall foliage, a visual splendour, is nature's right;
Rainbow with its fixed pattern of colours is an airy illusion
Foliage colours in fall is a real multicolour fest to vision.
As wounded soldiers leaves lie in gory red on the ground
after a display of bright colours in one full round.
Cheering smiles of cold lawns and green meadows
miss their greeting warmth as wily winter flows.
As mellowed sober sun imprints a warm kiss
Winter ushers as a silent thief with a cold hiss.
From the fleecy clouds races the cool rising moon
to hug the ravishing beauty of fall foliage soon.

Central Park

A vast seductive stretch of salubrious sylvan scene
spread with sunny sheets of levelled lushier lawn
in the heart of the human jungle in emerald sheen
the glittering green dons the ravishing robes of dawn.

Trees stand in regal charm in coloured cool costumes
green and red, pink and purple, yellow and vermillion
With glowing smiles of flowers the enchanting Eden blooms
With all these cast a sunny spell these leaves trillion.

Dotted with hilly rocks and teasing trekking tracks

rills gliding through highs and lows and craggy cracks
sky-high oaks, majestic maples and palmy rows of pines
stand in royal gait guarding pretty paths and lanes in lines.

Countless plants and creepers full with fragrant flowers
dance to the gliding breeze and greet Nature lovers;
Far from the moneyed frenzy of the multi-million crowd
shines Nature's foster child in green cover and cloud.

In the chosen centre of the world's economic epicentre
for hours and hours tired souls in thousands seek shelter;
This Central Park, a balmy cerebral park, Noah's novel arc
leads to peace and light far from oceanic din and dark.

Ice-Blocks Melt in Warm Love

Dear, I love to hear with my heart what you say
Our thoughts, free and fresh, so close often drift away
Our divergences as in a blind alley act and react
Vaguely straying away without adequate tact
While our convergences make us narrow
till we melt and dissolve to a big zero;
We shudder and shrink in freezing silence
and sink and stink in the trance of carnal lens;
Silence proves to be worse than violence.
Soon in minutes bubbles vanish and sky is clear
hearts clean and minds clear with a joyous tear.
In liberty we feel we sow, bloom and grow
But in reality our hearts moan and groan.
How restricted are our aimless thoughts
how conditioned are our minds and moves
it is beyond our mortal frame, it proves.
We are the slaves of our karma, the higher judge
the yawning gulf our acts alone can bridge;
Two different tracks are brought to meet
to make it broad, smooth and sweet
Soon there appears an apparent break
a figment of wild fancy, a momentary wreck;
All these barriers of ice-blocks melt in warm love
We know we are bonded slaves of ego
foolish victims languishing in self-erected iron towers
Thy painful loving looks drain all my energy
hurl us into the stagnated pool of lethargy

Our eyes grasp the subtle syntax of our looks
Now memory banishes its fangs of fire
wafts smiling breeze of mellowed melodic lyre
In storm and calm we cling and ring in love
and sail in a single boat hand in glove.

Random Reflections

As a boy at school I was spellbound
by the speech of a Senior College teacher
Like him I wished to be without a solid ground
From branch to branch I roamed with vague future
At last as a wind-driven boat I reached the English shore.
I like English, I like its cream and play and flights
It fed me as an affectionate foster mother
Along with mother tongue this kind alien angel
Guides my mind to unseen treasures and wild beauties
to wider vision, comprehensive look and depth of mind
I can't stoop to be a liar to say 'I am whoring with English Gods'
It has not chained my tongue, rather it has freed it
In fact I find joyous release and resurrecting relief
My tongue tastes the tongue and relishes its flavour and fragrance
While the essence of its classics and romantics is a feast to my mind;
Mother of mothers, Sanskrit shines for ever supreme
But I am not fortunate in this life to feel her divine touch
To explore the highest poetical flights and spiritual treasures
Can I transform my ailing autumn into spring?
I know this body in seventies can't go back to teens,
youth doesn't come back by wearing imported jeans;
but I could taste a few drops of its cherished honey
in the lines and letters of my sweet mother tongue.
From egoistic specifics and peevish particularities
I have journeyed to wider spaces and broad generalizations
No use in reviewing and leafing through the back pages
After a series of healers, feelers and time-driven estrangement
I learn to live in the moment, an inescapable fragment;
When into the smarting spaces of the past I can't descend,
into the foggy heights of future let me ascend.
Still I want to be still and feel myself young
Young in mind, young in thought and spirit to focus on the Lord
It makes me warm, works as a balm, lifts me up and fills the gap
With the tireless wings of an optimistic Siberian bird
I wish to fly beyond the lines and limits of ageing map

I wish to cross the insurmountable physical barrier
I hope to surmount with gritty committed career
No use in indulging in replay or in retrospect
Which makes us sink in non-descript regret
Without looking back better to march to bright prospect
The more we look behind the longer the pain it begets
The days I live I live to learn about the Supreme Lord
think of the Ultimate Truth and sing on His glory as a bard
and try to step on the right path to reach the Eternal.

Selected Criticism

When Grief Rains - Review by Dr. D.C. Chambial

T.V. Reddy is now a familiar name in Indian English poetry. *When Grief Rains* is his maiden book of verses wherein an ardent reader of poetry can discern poet's particular sensibility of brooding melancholy at the face of this world full of its sick hurry and divided aims.

'Dream' is a realistic poem that gives vent to the poet's unrealized dreams, in a delightful manner. The poet affirms:

> So many dreams
> have dried up in my heart
> like beads of tears
> on the burning cheeks

and is powerful enough to draw reader's sympathy by means of a sensuous image. The poet seems diffident in facing the reality when he writes 'I dread the yet unborn progeny/ and flee from the reflected agony' and wishes to escape 'from these ills/ and enter the pores of the earth'. For, the poet does not decipher 'where the darkness leads to'. In 'Transience' the poet infers that the human life and all its efforts are insignificant.

> Great deeds are written in water,
> All glories lead only to dust.

'My Wish' a short lovely piece, exhibits poet's anguish and anger passionately and the reader sits upright to know why the poet wishes

> to spin the dirty disc;
> this earth, and hurling
> it at the clouded sky.

The contemplative sensibility of the poet becomes more and more dismal as the poet marches ahead. For the poet death is the only solution to all problems of this life: 'The exit of the gasping breath alone/ shall release me from the lingering pain' and this life: The exit of the gasping breath alone/ shall release me from the lingering pain' and this life, for the poet, is 'A tedious journey over the soil through the dust.... an endless desert...a gruesome game full of stink and stench/ with neither sunshine nor raindrops to guide to the shore'. The poet's pessimism culminates in as he writes 'Death is the only reality/dust is the only eternity'. Though it is eternal truth, yet hope sustains life. Deserts too have oases.

In "Sweet Sear" the poet observes:

> Now I realize:
> when that dream dissolves,
> the pensive memory of the scar-+
> on the wounded heart
> is tastier....

Here the poet is echoing John Keats's "consciousness of mutability" as experienced in his 'Ode on Melancholy'.

The predominant note in the book is one of gloom, pessimism, disillusion, frustration and melancholy and the poet finds solace only in death. The poet has used images, symbols and alliteration to heighten the tonal effect. The lines are crisp. The style is perfectly simple and lucid. Clarity of thought, lucidity of style and sincerity of expression appeal to the reader most. Had Reddy cared a bit more to swing his poetic sensibility towards the brighter side of life, he would have attained a new height. The poet's melancholy is mellowed by emotional and imaginative sharing of the hard nudities of the time. Every poem is a nugget of thoughtful fancy studded in the fabric of poet's pageant of poetic filigree.

(published in Poetry, Vol XII, No.1, 1987, p.135)

Broken Rhythms - Editor's Note by Dr. Krishna Srinivas

Dr. T. Vasudeva Reddy is a morning star in the firmament of Indo-Anglian poetry. He is a poet par excellence who has profound message to convey. He gives articulation to human struggle and unrest, social as well as psychological, and depicts restlessness that is the order of modern times. To him life is a field of algebra but he wants to be "himself without any dissembling".

With Baudelarian frankness he protests against the social ills & evils and cries down the cruelty to our fellowmen. He exposes pseudo Swamijis who drink "pure milk and juice brought by fair sex", plundering leaders and terrorists on their spree. He sings memorable lines.

> The genii of this wondrous earth
> with the power of all their years
> dare not touch the rim of cosmos
> nor traverse a wink of light year.

In "My soul's plea" he gives expression to powerful emotions and blazing imagination:

> Do not stop me
> I should be uncontrollable
> As thy Bay of Bengal
> Do not remove the ashes
> Lest the embers of my soul
> Should sparkle and blaze forth
> I am the eclipsed sun
> And the moth near the lamp

His "New Year's Day" is a remarkable poem for its pensive and reflective mood which forces everyone to look back and look before:

> On the slippery road of eternal life
> I have crossed many milestones
> that make my bare feet bleed

In fact the present collection is remarkable for its wide range of themes and interests. His poems are a great contribution to the treasure of world poetry. Life is not replete with despair and anguish alone; the other side also beams with lasting joys and enthusiasm. In his next collection I feel sure he will give a covetous bunch of poems both memorable and solacing.

(published as Editor's Note to the collection *The Broken Rhythms*)

Fleeting Bubbles - Review by A. Russell (poet & critic, London):

The Fleeting Bubbles is a thin sheaf of 'occasional' verses from T. Vasudev Reddy whose love for writing poetry is a celebrated adventure in the domain of Indo-English production of our times.

Should we say that he is a strong visualist often engaged in a craft to create the scene and situation where he can posit his 'poetic self' to say and to react? There is sufficient reason to believe so:

> Beneath the pale peepal tree
> by the fast-drying pond
> in that double roasted hamlet
> Woman stand like expiring candles.

Image-packed a scene is built up with little strain and some felicity; only that his syntax is a bit strained, phrasing no less laboured. The import of his lines comes off; straight away he gives away without any attempt of concealing what he needs to state. So by the time you are at the last line you can walk off with the bloc of sensibility inscribed into your psyche.

In short poems where the statement dominates, rather constituting the nucleus, what he says is given a poetry form, clarity becomes grace, and no lapses in craft can mar the art of being genuine and frank about one's feelings. The control over syntax is commendable if not perfect.

> I fled from you, from me and all
> I thought so, but alas !
> I found myself amid you
> like a frightened cat.

Stock images do not sound jaded in such situations; even they acquire edge, the ability to encapsulate feelings. In 'Agony' he is poignant and phrases are composed to a rare control. A remarkable feature of his self exposition is that he is not sentimental anywhere.

'I am tired' is a self-exploration that rises to an acme of pathos without being self-indulgent or cathetic. He keeps his prose by tightening up the structure sprucely composed, some poems reveal that he has trained his mind on saying things in a poetic fashion. Even the jejune sound interesting and the drably familiar acquires a halo of mystery.

Though he writes in English he does not anglicize his thoughts. Nor does he hide his emotions as the pseudo-English so often do in the worn-out fashion of neo-metaphysicals. He remains a native, an Indian in what he thinks about the world in its enigmatic appeal, a pantheist at the core of his heart. His is stuff with a distinctly Indian flavour, the ripe jackfruit and appetizing yellow of mango in a basket.

(Published in Poetry Time, No.1&2, 1990)

Melting Melodies - Review by Dr. Dwarakanath H. Kabadi

Poetry is turning out to be an industry. With talent or without talent poems are being manufactured as consumer goods and more often than not most of the poems end up in the dustbin. May be the urge to become one more mighty Milton or a noble Tagore might be the driving force for this unwieldy production of this pedestrian in poetry.

The book in review by Dr. T. Vasudeva Reddy is quite an exception for the reason that the poems in this slim collection have the earthly smear of sweat and blood. Images crystallized, come alive in subtle but strong words gaining a permanent place in the heart of the readers.

Dr. Reddy, as I have seen him, is a tower of humility and a flower of divinity. The life he has seen encompasses all aspects, roots going deep into the native soil from which he himself has emerged; with its customs and culture intact it makes him paint true life stories. His poems cover from social imbalances to satanic wars, from historical events to archeological ruins, from human greed to Godly deeds. His pen moves carving lasting images in a simple and straight form without any pompous gimmicks in the name of modern craft.

Melting Melodies surely melts but not in the heat, but in one's heart. Many poems carrying the weight of empathy become one with the toiler, but sharp swords to the exploiter and the traitor:

> Is there scarcely a heart that sighs for your sweat (The Tiller.p.8)
> Barrels of liquor fail to quench the thirst
> of our pot-bellied leaders   (Thirst -p.9)

> His ideal has been to bury the nation's ideals
> which he gave up ages ago
> 'Save thyself and serve none'   (Our Leader-p.11)

> Every piece of ruin, a marvel of art
> in stone/carves a mute message
> a chose of a faded epic/each tiny
> speck/an iridescent luminous spark   (The Fort-p.5)

His craftsmanship in painting his experiences in words with different images makes them remain in our memories to haunt us for a long time. Words dance to the tune of thoughts and create deafening sounds, but in total silence. Melodies that reverberate into the pits of silence linger and stay stronger: 'The Toiling Woman', 'Thirst', 'Our Leaders', 'A Bubble', and many more poems are evocative and many end with a poignant note of the futility of life and immortality of pain and exploitation: ill-gotten wealth/ Growing like elephantiasis is touching but true.

His art of highlighting even tiny specks into gigantic monuments and the quality of lyrical writing gives a sense of exhilaration bringing the varied themes alive before our eyes elevating the soul to a higher consciousness both when in tears as well as in joyous outbursts. Thus he builds a fort from his words and quietly imprisons our thoughts unawares to ponder over life.

his spells out the unique beauty of the poetry of T.V.Reddy and his poems bear a strong testimony to their intrinsic charm and charming melody. Indeed T.V. Reddy is a poet in the true sense, who gives us the best of the poetry in Indian English, and I am sure many more worthy works will emerge from his ever sensitive pen.

(Pubd. in *Poetcrit*, Jan.1996, pp.52-54 & recently in *Writers, Editors Critics* (GIEWEC Jl.) Vol.7, No.1, Mar. 2017, pp.112-113; ISBN 2231-198X)

Pensive Memories - Review by Dr. Atma Ram

Pensive Memories is T. Vasudeva Reddy's fifth Collection of poems. It contains his 40 poems, 35 haiku, and carries an elaborate Foreword by Prof. Nissim Ezekiel. The poet has been a teacher and Principal at the college and university level and won several coveted awards and honours in creative art and education. A world level writer of great repute, he has also done two novels, two critiques on Jane Austen and a book on English Grammar.

Poems in the *Pensive Memories*, we are told, are results of a "long choosing and beginning late." The poet has been composing these when he was, may one say, "in pensive or in vacant mood". These are simple, straight and short pieces charged with intensity and passion. Reddy dwells on various themes and scenes but often links them all by a note of sad musings. One feels a lure for the next one as one goes through them; one wishes to read on-and-on, go to the next and the next. The anthology begins with 'The New Year'. The year has ended, leaving behind it 'bleak memories and unfulfilled desires', and the poet looks forward to the New Year with hope and zest: 'May it brighten the days with melodic lyres.' "Can I Sing" lays bare the inherent pain and misery of the poet. In the midst of tension and trouble, he can't sing or dance, churn out sober ideas or paint vivid scenes. Nor can he die peacefully:

> Can I die
> a quiet and peaceful death
> with a mind full of cares
> and body full

To examine a few more poems: In "The Bridal Bosom" the far off clouds inspire the poet to leap and hop, whereas in "Bride's Wishes" he portrays beautifully the bride's vision of 'the unseen spheres of joy.' "An Orphan Lad" and "Migrating Birds" touchingly describe the plight of the lowliest and the lost; in "The Crow", Reddy concentrates on the crow who symbolically reminds him of the values of the hoary past:

> 'But you embody values extinct in man
> Thy cry is free from our corrupt note.'

In "The Dull Evening" the poet is in the mood of inertia and indolence, when "Sailing Saree" conjures up a romantic scene. One is tempted to examine more and more poems of enduring charm and beauty.

However, the most effective songs of haunting nature pertain to the sad , untimely demise of T.V. Reddy's wife. The title poem "Pensive Memories" is at once short yet heart-touching. The poet concentrates on what is gone and what is left behind, and each line vibrates with a melody of its own:

> The sudden exit of my half, my better half
> Leaves the other a deserted fragmented self
> The present stands aloof as an odious outcaste.

A viable movement from "graces to ashes'. But he cheers up and confidently asserts in the 'Power of Love': 'It is an end, but not the end.' In several other songs, the great loss is tersely echoed – for instance, in "To My Other Half", "Without You", "A Pair of Doves" and "Waiting".

In some other pieces, T.V. Reddy opens up and treats adequately wider themes of human interest and concern. He depicts the confounded state of modern man in "Unpredictable Man", one who is 'at once a man and a monster'. This world is an illusion, a play – Maya. To the poet pious actions and pure thoughts, therefore, matter the most. He observes:

> Beads and beards can't save you
> Neither billions nor bullions too
> Pure thought or a small good act
> saves you and ensures His grace in fact.   ('Save Thyself')

In "Sabari" Reddy narrates a famous episode in *The Ramayana*. In 'Tsunami' he paints in heart-rending word-images the picture of terrible tidal wave, and a colossal natural calamity that occurred on 26 Dec. 2004 in South East Asia. Haiku (35 in number) given in the end of the anthology express ideas directly and unequivocally. Like Arjuna's arrows, the three-line verses hit the nail on the head. To a large extent, a common man's perception effectively communicated, bluntly laid bare. What do our political masters promise? Answers Reddy, with a note of irony:

> We want your ballots
> you are sure to get bullets
> from our bullet-proof cars.

And this time, no enhancement in D.A., please, because –

> This time no D.A. to N.G.Os
> We are not free from woes
> To our vote bank money flows.

An implicit yet hard-hitting comment on anti-dowry (or dowry) campaign:

> He gave a loud talk against dowry
> the place resounded with full applause
> he received ten million, his son's dowry.

Dr. Reddy is essentially a teacher. The present reviewer remembers having met him in a UGC National Seminar two decades ago – a government college lecturer bubbling with vigour and vitality. (Sincerely condole his wife's death and suggest him to study books like *Life is Fair: The Law of Cause and Effect* by Brian Hines, Radha Soami Satsang Beas, Dera Baba Jaimal Singh, District Amritsar – 143204). His poetry has something common with several other teacher-poets such as Kanwar Dinesh Singh, M.L. Kaul, L.M. Sharma, Suman Sachar, L.R. Nagpal, PCK Prem, R.K. Singh, D.C. Chambial and Nalini Sharma: traits of clarity and digested literary allusions or echoes. The poet in *Pensive Memories* knows what he knows and invariably conveys that in vivid and conspicuous language. As an instructor, Reddy must have taught numerous poems including so many elegies. His poetry points to their influence or awareness. However everything has been naturally absorbed in his literary art and his 'sad' memories embody pattern and rhythm of their own. They appeal us tremendously, as they, in general, incorporate "the saddest thought."

Well-known for his poetic images, variety of themes and sweep of vision, Reddy is surely at his best in *Pensive Memories*. Many poems irresistibly haunt the reader as the content and form are finely knit together. Here the sound often seems to echo the sense.

In sum, the collection of poems is slender in size but very significant in importance. Surely, one agrees with Prof. Nissim Ezekiel that "here melodies really melt and flow with a quiet beauty and pensive charm. It marks steady development of thought and full maturity of the poetic process." It is an excellent specimen of Indian English Poetry. I believe that the genre, despite the croaking detractors, richly deserves as in-depth critical assessment in terms of book-length studies and doctoral dissertations.

Dr. Atma Ram is an Eminent Academician, Critic and Educationist. Retired as Education Adviser to Govt. of H.P. & Director of Higher Ed., HP. Published in *Poetcrit*, Jan.2007; pp.116-119. Reprinted with permission.

Gliding Ripples - Review by Dr. K. Rajani

Gliding Ripples is the sixth book of poems written by T. Vasudeva Reddy, popularly as T.V. Reddy in literary circles. He needs no introduction as he is a well-known poet and all his previous five collections of poems beginning with *When Grief Rains* (Delhi, Samakaleen, 1982) bear a strong testimony to the remarkable poetic calibre and the creative genius of Dr. T.V. Reddy. No wonder, now he is one of the leading lights of Indian poetry in English. The present volume is an extension of the dimensions of the creative art of his poetry.

Gliding Ripples is an exciting bunch of 57 poems comprising Part I and a hundred haiku comprising Part II and the poems encompass a wide range of experience and subject matter from books to national leaders and borders, from impoverished villages to falling bridges, from roses and rainbows to mosquitoes and pigeons and from our renowned heritage site Mahabalipuram to American life and the world-famous Niagara Falls. The scope of this poetry collection is indeed amazing and its range is ravishingly wide and varied. The collection begins with the thought-provoking poem 'Erase the Borders' which fills our minds with disturbing waves and shocking sounds of guns and speeding bullets. The thematic relevance of the poem is as rich and profound as its glowing message:

> Boundaries exist only in mind
> whipped up by theories blind;
> Let us not race for winning runs,
> in one voice wipe out killing guns;
> emotions rise in cricket mall,
> but let not a pawn or a wicket fall.

The next poem 'What is there for Pride' is purely philosophical expressing the transitory nature of human life and the inescapable reality of death and the meaningless nature of pride:

> What is there for human pride?
> Pages red with pitiless helpless blood
> darkened with its streaming flood...   (p.12)

The next one "Mortuary of Books' is indeed an unforgettable poem for its vitriolic satire, pungent humour and impenetrable irony and it is no exaggeration to say that it is one of our best poems in the realm of English poetry. Books in most of our libraries stay untouched and lie undisturbed:

> Books fail to seduce cold eunuchs,
> sigh and lie undisturbed in Yogic sleep
> like innocent babes in engraved cradles.

The library gives the impression of a mortuary; as such see the fate of the precious books preserved in the library:

> Is it a mortuary of books
> guarded by white ants, spiders and flies
> or a place of moths, lice and butterflies
> to roam, gossip and exchange looks
> or a domed Taj to spell academic doom?   (p.14)

The next poem 'Idols for the Idle' is equally interesting and intellectually stimulating and it gives a graphic sketch of the deterioration of values in the modern times by presenting the olden days when statues of really great and worthy persons were installed while in the modern day people compete in installing the statues of corrupt persons, underworld dons and criminals. The poem 'Our Bureaucrat' gives a realistic sketch of most of the present day bureaucrats who are mostly corrupt. While the lines on the ideal life of Rama focus our attention on the building up of noble character, the poem 'A Mother's Cry' reveal the depth of mother's love for her children and her greater love for the son who is snatched away from her by the hungry sea.

The poem 'The Bridge' overflows with the social consciousness of the poet T.V. Reddy who succeeds in exposing the enormity of corruption in every walk of life and here he gives an instance of a newly constructed bridge across a river:

> It is built afresh to act
> as a peacemaker with tact....
> of sand on sand with sand to stand
> till the issue of cheque to withstand.   (p.66)

'Our Leader' is a short piece presenting a typical present day political leader with striking imagery, clarity and surgical precision:

> Crowds as flocks did follow
> his fat white-clad shadow,
> thicker than his gory riches,
> taller than his free promises. (p.68)

One of the most interesting poems in this volume is 'Oh, America!' and the poem is at once an appreciation of the high advancement of the country and the cleanliness and an exposure of the sky-high charges of medical treatment:

> If you yourself, by any lapse, fail to insure
> Your life's boat is sure to sink, be sure;
> If you fall critically ill and on evil days
> 'Fly to India, wise man of the East says;
> Surgical or spiritual care costs very least,
> The sun sets in the west only to rise in the east.   (pp.75-76)

The haiku part is equally interesting and qualitative and I dare say T.V. Reddy is one of our best haikuists and his haiku far surpass those of the other writers because of the extraordinary care in creating these miniature poems, and each haiku emerges from his pen as a pearl by itself. There is not only clarity, compactness and compression of thought, there is the beauty of the rhythm which is rare indeed:

> World is wide/ for the youth to ride/on the crest of tide. (p.83)
> With smiling pearls/you make my life bloom -/the spring chases gloom.(p.83)
> With a drop of tea/ the heavy heart feels free -/a cloudless sky.
> Our universities,/ large academic slums -/ political drums. (p. 92)
> One tender smile/ lights many a mile,/ eases an uphill task. (p.94)

Thus the collection *Gliding Ripples* as a whole is a solid proof of the poetic potentiality and social consciousness of T.V. Reddy. While some of the poems reveal his potential for projecting the sharp satirical element, a few more poems reveal him as a nature poet. His presentation of the contemporary village life has few parallels indeed. All the poems without a single exception are quite remarkable for their incisive thought and freshness of content and expression.

(published in *Bizz Buzz* (Bangalore), vol.15; 2012; pp.123-127.)

Quest for Peace – Note by Prof. Jaydeep Sarangi, Kolkata

Quest for Peace: A Minor Social Epic is a veritable and engaging image gallery that engages a reader to sit and read in one sitting. It is a poetic account of 'soul's ceaseless flight'. Various influences, Indian mythological past, poetic subjectivity, and otherwise, went into the making of a vibrant poet of contemporary India. His lines evoke a subtle comparison, namely between the body as a place of desire and that of an actual shelter as the place of home and sweet heart.

Reddy is a socially engaged poet for whom a poem is a sociological commitment: 'Let us free this city from heat and hunger.' A committed poet goes back to the nostalgic past and dingy days of the White Raj. The poem has a satiric bend. Reddy is blunt like many other contemporary poets from the mainland or North-East: 'after all our leaders, blind to the public pulse.' His deft use of words and phrases in conveying the subtle nuances of meaning is the highlight of his poetry. The poet's frank and sharp lexicon is his forte. The holy Ganga flows like sweet cadence in a beautiful social epic where we are taken on in a journey to the sublime.

Golden Veil – Review by Bernard M. Jackson

> From pensive past rooted in pain and penury
> I march through varied shades and scars of injury;
> From the clouds of rage and envy I emerge like a star,
> Let me stand erect and soar upright and fly afar;

Soaring above the clouds of regrets and total neglect
I hope to leave a few humble lyrical notes to recollect.

(Let Me Stand Erect)

Tirupati-born poet, and critic and novelist of already considerable national and international renown, Dr. T. Vasudeva Reddy, in the years following a most impressive scholastic career as a Senior University lecturer, leading to becoming Principal of the Govt. Degree College (2001), was later to achieve outstanding acclaim from the Michael Madhusudan Dutt Academy (Calcutta) in 1994, for his third published poetry collection, *The Fleeting Bubbles*. And four years later, this was to be followed by the prestigious UGC Award of National Fellowship. Nissim Ezekiel, a prominent Mumbai critic, tells us: 'T.V. Reddy is always a realist and his poems are reflection of his socio-economic consciousness.... Like a gifted sculptor he chisels his poems with the deftness of a master craftsman ....'

Certainly, T.V. Reddy's poems are imbued with great perceptive insight, are vivid in portrayal, and substantial in attendant imagery. His crafted works evince not only smoothness of pace, but ascend to lyrical heights of literary magnitude. Despite his advancement of professional status, T. V. Reddy remains exceedingly proud of his immediate family's former humble circumstances, and indeed there is revealing reference, in one of his poems, to his father's remembered school conditions in the village where he had lived: "It was an open school beside an earthen street, / Where cows would low and sheep would bleat / Under the open sky that served as school vault" (My Father's School Days).

The poet speaks with heart-rending compassion about the disastrous plight of his fellow country folk, in those typical rural circumstances, during the intensive heat of summer, when water is so desperately needed:

Old man like autumnal leaves wither
while parched birds reel, droop and drop;
streets, spilling heat, wear a deserted look.
Fields crack as farmers' hearts crack.
Monsoon loves to play hide and seek,
Crops die a dismal death as aborted babies,
Women walk miles for a pot of water.
In towns, bikes run with water cans,
Cattle perish in hunger and acute thirst.
As summer sizzles, our hearts boil and burst. (Summer Sizzles)

There is much sagacity within T. V. Reddy's writings, and of course, this is only to be expected of one who had been so prominent n the field of higher education. Hence, many of his poems will have a decidedly didactic appeal for most readers:

> Live in Nature, live with Nature,
> Move in Nature, merge with Nature.
> Nature is our mother and teacher,
> nurse, guide, friend and preacher.
> Let us be content with her gifts and fruits,
> varieties of vegetables and lusty leaves.
> Let us rely on the wealth of edible roots;
> Doubtless, us in pink of health she leaves. (Nature)

There are love poems, too, and with these there are accompanying references to the sad personal loss of a loved one - Perhaps, quite a number of years ago:

> Before these pale eyes, you incarnate on the page,
> Coming alive as a gentle wave to inspire me as a sage;
> Words on the letter belong to the pale fading page
> and limp through decades till this withering stage. (The Letter)

However, the poem that pleased me most, within this fine collection, was, 'Birthday Function'. And reading this poem aloud, one is there 'in a grand decorated hall in the luxury three-star hotel.' The contained imagery within this poem is so vividly expressed, and T.V. Reddy's lines of verse are exquisitely enhanced with a musicality engendered by crafted turn of word and phrase:

> Bunches of helium balloons dispelled the cloud of tedium;
> Pizza and dosa served many a young and aged palette
> The processed and the fresh with their mixed tastes
> pleased all the tongues and dishes didn't go waste.
> Birthday song, the paid piper amid claps did sing;

All blank heads joined, and the chorus did ring. (Birthday Function)

There are, within the collection, a number of sonnets which, though deviating from the more usual decasyllabic mode, are nevertheless beautifully presented. "Eternal Ethics" by far the best of these and, incidentally, T. V. Reddy's concluding poem, provides powerful spiritual finalisation to the collection as a whole. This is Indian-English poetry at its very best, and Reddy is a gifted writer whose profound work I feel it is my great honour to have had to review.

(pubd. in PoetCrit, Jan. - June 2017, pp.161-'2)

Thousand Haiku Pearls – Review by Patricia Prime

Professor T. Vasudeva Reddy is a renowned poet, critic and novelist. His poems have appeared in French journals and he received the "Excellence in World Poetry" award in 2009. In his Preface to Thousand Haiku Pearls, Professor Reddy states: "It is a well-known fact that haiku is the Japanese mode of mini-poetic form with a tight poetic structure of three lines following 5-7-5 syllabic structure." Reddy has also introduced rhyme into his haiku as he feels: "I tried to breathe rhyme into this miniature form thereby lending melody and dignity to it."

Unlike most of the haiku being written in the Western canon, Professor Reddy's haiku retain devices most of us have dropped: his poems begin with a capital and end with a period and retain the lengthier 5-7-5-count. The opening capital emphasizes the event to follow and draws attention to the moment, while the period acts as a closure to the haiku. The lengthy lines draw and open the poem to space and flow, while the rhyme contributes to the melody of the haiku. Reddy says that although the book is titled *Thousand Haiku Pearls*, it contains one thousand and eight haiku "since this is the mostly chosen number of our traditional Indian poets and seers from ancient times."

The haiku are real; neither clever nor brilliant, but more important to this reviewer, they are soulful. Consider the following two haiku, which one can easily relate to the plight of refugees in modern times:

> Tears on the road –
> the unclaimed orphan child,
> the victim of terror wild. (p.11)

> The endless ethnic war
> spreads on the race a shroud –
> a dark cloud. (p.11)

Details in the poems pull the reader into them. From there, the impressions continue as long as the reader wishes to linger. Although these particular haiku are a challenge, they do not prevent Reddy from enjoying nature, as the following verses indicate:

> Drops of dew,
> Nature's gift, our delight –
> Priceless pearls bright. (p.16)

> Sunset in shower
> in cave-like leafy bower
> hides the little bird. (p.25)

Many of the poems in this volume are not necessarily about nature. The poet gives us glimpses of the city, politics, doctors, schools, trains, pubs and violence. The book is filled with poems which continue to resonate after repeated readings and these powerful haiku communicate an understated elegance. The haiku often shine with a sudden seeing—but while moments of insight might be the stock in trade of the haiku poet, what might be more surprising is the realization of their relevance to our modern world. In these haiku we are shown the poet's environs, the people he encounters, and their relationship of these things to the poet and his writing. What emerges is a sense of patterning which, recurring, offers the engaged reader a way out of the mundane, a moving towards peace and tranquillity:

> I stand on the beach
> listening to waves that preach
> the eternal gospel. (p.34)

> The river at last flows
> consoles the people and glows
> in their parched eyes.(p.35)

There are other threads to follow as well: the sense of the land, children and the winter sun, as we see in the following haiku:

> Evening rays of the sun
> kiss the stretch of ripened rice field,
> the golden yield. (p.40)

> Ball falls and rises
> Boys eager to play and win prizes
> World is a playfield. (p.40)

> The winter sun
> invites us with a mild balmy cool,
> flowers and leaves are one. (p.43)

In the haiku we see a connectedness which all creatures in the world share—the call for change in our politics and ideas, our relationship with fellow creatures, and our need to take care of the planet and each other, collectively our sense of being at home with ourselves.

> Search for seeds
> in modern minds full of weeds –
> a futile exercise. (p. 57)

> Others let us not hurt
> Words have power to thrill or kill of heal
> Let the thrust be on others' weal. (p. 58)

Subtle, elegant, profound, Reddy's haiku broadens his unwavering focus on the natural and the modern world and turn them inwards to explore the complex realm of the human and the divine. As he exhorts:

> Let us be conscious
> of the One Divine in us, the most precious,
> to spread the Kingdom of God. (p.66)

Whether he is describing the boundless sky, nature's varied ranges, or the lack of water and the way they affect both human and animal life as presented in -

> No water in the lake,
> Physical thirst it can't slake;
> Frogs leave the place. (p.72)

or the sight of children playing, or his passage through life, Reddy is a writer of plainspoken reverence:

> It is the moment
> that decides the future to bloom
> or we perish in gloom. (p.81)

> We are impure;
> With this heavy baggage, the sinful load
> we can't cross the road. (p.132)

This book presents a thousand and eight haiku, whose effect is like afternoon light hitting ordinary objects and extraordinary subjects: it illuminates, clarifies, and directs our gaze toward what it is we love and respect and to those things of which we sometimes despair. It explores the mysteries of life, with the greatest mystery of them all creeping ever closer. He sings our sorrows and our joys. Nothing escapes his notice and in this sequence of individual haiku, he has mapped the world of shadows found among our everyday lives.

(pubd. in *Writers Editors Critics*, Sept. 2016, pp.131-133)

Conversations with T.V. Reddy

Interview with Prof. A.K. Chowdary, Editor, *Kohinoor*

From *Kohinoor*, Vol.12, 2012; ISSN-0973-6395; pp.1-5) Pubd. By Prof. A.K. Choudhary, Assam, India. Reprinted with permission.

AKC: When did you first consider yourself a writer?
TVR: As a matter of fact I considered myself a writer, of course, in my own innocent way, during the last days of my high school life when I began writing poems in English under the guidance of my father, a school teacher. During my college life my poems in English were published in the university college magazine.

AKC: What inspired you to write your first book?
 TVR: My first book happened to be a poetry book *When Grief Rains* (Delhi, Samakaleen Prakashan, 1982) a collection of poems. Though I was writing short poems, I had not published till then. Two or three years before that, I had the opportunity of going through two anthologies of Indian poetry in English, one by R. Parthasarathy and the other by Pritish Nandy. After reading those verses I seriously thought why I should not continue to write poems and get them published. I felt I could write better poems than most of the pieces published in them. That gave me confidence and that competitive spirit inspired me to write poetry in English.

AKC: What books have influenced your life most?
TVR: Of course, as the son of the soil my life was much influenced by *The Ramayana* and *The Mahabharata* which have moulded me to some extent. But as a writer in English, I was very much influenced by the Romantic poets Wordsworth, Keats and Shelley. As regards fiction, I like Jane Austen's *Pride and Prejudice*, Charles Dickens's *Hard Times* and Hardy's *The Woodlanders*. Wordsworth's shorter poems "Daffodils" and "Solitary Reaper," Keats's *Odes* and Shelley's "Ode to the West Wind", "To a Skylark" and "The Cloud", simply enchant me with the beauty of nature, richness of emotion and simplicity of expression wherein lies their greatness.

AKC: Do you have a specific writing style?

TVR: I don't have any specific writing style. But as far as possible, I want my expression in poetry as well as in novel to be closer to nature and truth and so to be simple and clear, free from ambiguity.

AKC: Is there anything you find particularly challenging in your writing?

TVR: In most of my poems as well as my novels, I have taken up the presentation of the true picture of the typical Indian village life as a challenging task, because I did not find that aspect of life given due attention. Almost all the writers with their highly urbanized life in metropolitan cities do not have any first-hand knowledge of the present day village life and by making one or two picnic trips to the countryside they feel vain glorious in presenting the scanty surface picture of what they have seen in one or two days or a week at the most. Unless the writer is born and brought up in the village and continues to live in the village he cannot grasp the roots of the rural life; that is why I consider it a challenging task to present the reality of village life.

AKC: What is your favourite theme or element in writing?

TVR: Presenting the truth of rural life without any falsification or artificiality is my chosen theme. I live in the village, my roots are in the village, my soul is in the village and as such I can confidently depict the rural life with all its merits and demerits. Exploitation of the poor by the rich landlords is one side of the good old picture which most of the stereotyped writers relish to present as they are unfortunately unaware of the other side of the picture i.e. the exploitation of the rich by the poor and the poor by the poor which is indeed the order of the day now. Most of the writers are deliberately blind to this stark reality which is the bitter truth .

AKC: Who is your favourite author and what is it that really strikes you about their work?

TVR: It is a very difficult to answer this question, because I like very much one or two poets, one or two novelists, and a playwright as they belong to different genres. Let me confess Shakespeare is my favourite author, while Keats my favourite poet. In Shakespeare, we are face-to-face with the totality of human nature and move in a living world of men and matters, while some of the poems of Keats stir our feelings and kindle our emotions. I move with Prince Hamlet in his inner world sharing his refined feelings and noble sentiments, and at the same time I wish to share the solitude of Keats partaking the glory of his imaginary poetic flights.

AKC: Where do you get most of the ideas?

TVR: Firmly rooted in the village, I draw my inspiration from nature and, as such, ideas as well as themes, springing from nature and human nature, pour into my mind. Moreover my village is situated between two rivers close to the forest that covers the Seshachala Hills or Tirumala Hills on the top of which the renowned Temple of Lord Venkateswara is located. What the Lake District was to Wordsworth, my native locality is to me. Moreover, as I belong to the village and as I am also a marginal farmer I know the problems of small farmers and peasants and the true colours of the two sides of exploitation and corruption. Nowadays a village Panchayat is more or less like our capital New Delhi in miniature bustling with political activity and Machivellian diplomacy. No wonder, most of our leaders come from the village background. It supplies all the ideas to a good observer.

AKC: How do you choose the names of your characters?
TVR: Generally this point of choosing names doesn't arise in writing poems. Even when a few characters are sketched, the poet tries to generalize and universalize them and in such a situation giving a particular name to the character becomes an obstacle to the progress of the poetic thought. But while writing a novel or short story or a play the process of naming characters assumes greater significance. For my novels and short stories I chose names keeping in view their role, their action and thematic background. In this context the Hindu epics and my cultural background come to my help in giving names to my fictional characters.

AKC: What is your favourite character archetype of literature?
TVR:-Without any second thought, Prince Hamlet; he is everyman on the positive side. Indeed Shakespeare created Hamlet as an archetypal character; in him we see all the virtues and noble qualities. He is a great genius who falls a victim to adverse circumstances and to the unkind fate before which all his merits and great virtues, his extraordinary intelligence and imagination, his majesty and magnanimity unfortunately fail thereby bringing an abrupt end to a brilliant career.

AKC: What scene in your writing has made you laugh the hardest or cry the most ?
TVR: The scene of celebration of Krishnaiah's daughter Jyothi's marriage with Gopal in my second novel *Minor Gods* makes me laugh and at the same time cry at the greed of Durga the groom's mother who insists that unless the bride's father gives on the spot an additional amount for the purchase of a scooter her son would not tie the Mangalasuthra. Such incidents are not uncommon even in today's society which is still haunted by the dowry system. Though the system now seems in one way to be on the wane, it has increased in another way intensifying the anxiety and the threat to the safety of the newly married girl.

AKC: Who do you act out the scenes in your novels with?

TVR: I appreciate the role of Govindaiah the village postmaster who remains a good friend, guide and philosopher to Krishnaiah his friend and relative through thick and thin steadfastly till the end instilling courage and confidence, hope and solace. He is a balanced and ethical person with right thinking capable of giving right advice in any situation however critical it is. He is a true friend to Krishnaiah and a real guide to Pratap and to his daughter Latha. With such persons we can hope to restore order in the society.

AKC: What is your favourite novel by a different author?

TVR: I like Hardy's Tess. Hardy's delineation of Tess as a pure character though she lost her virginity is superbly done. In the re-creation of Wessex rural background Hardy is simply unsurpassed and the presentation of Tess's psychological struggle in her choice between Angel Clare and Alex is really touching. Hardy succeeds in getting our sympathy for her. It becomes difficult to forget her and therein lies the greatness of Hardy.

AKC: Do you have any advice for other writers?

TVR: I just wish to share my honest ideas with other modest writers of my kind. Whether it is poetry or fiction we should be honest in thought and expression and whatever we present should as far as possible be realistic; we should be true to nature and being nature's children we should never ignore the power and influence of nature. Moreover, as responsible members of our society, we as writers have a higher responsibility to look at men and matters with an unbiased outlook and present the same in clear and simple expression so as to make people see the reality and rectify the errors by taking corrective steps instead of bowing to personal prejudices, narrow ideas and corrupt practices. So let us not care for shallow awards and hollow recognition and let us spread the message of human dignity, morality and concern for fellow human beings.

Interview with Santanu Halder, *Kolkata (28-Feb-2013)*

Dr. T. Vasudeva Reddy occupies a significant place in Indian literary circles. His poems unveil the inner essence of life. Born in December 1943 in a village near Tirupati, he did masters in English in 1966; got his Ph. D for his thesis on the novels of Jane Austen. He worked as lecturer, reader and UGC National Fellow and visiting Professor, and retired as Principal of a Government degree college in December 2001.

He received the Awards of International Eminent Poet in 1987, Hon. D. Litt. from the WAAC, San Francisco in 1988, Best Teacher Award at the College & University level from the Govt. of AP in 1990, Best Poetry award for his third poetry book *The Fleeting Bubbles* from Michael Madhusudan Dutt Academy, Calcutta in 1994 and the prestigious U.G.C Award of National Fellowship in 1998.

His biography figures in the American Biographical Institute (N. Carolina, USA), International Biographical Institute (Cambridge), Reference India and Asia (New Delhi), and Sahitya Akademi (New Delhi). He is a renowned poet, critic and novelist of international repute. His poems appeared in French journals in Paris. M.Phil and Ph.D. theses have been produced on his works. Recently, he received the international Award of "Excellence in World Poetry" in 2009.

In a candid conversation with citizen journalist Shantanu Haldar, Dr Reddy speaks about his passion for poetry. Excerpts.

Can you define poetry in your own words?

It is very difficult to define poetry. It is easier to say what is not a poem than to say what really is a good poem. Nowadays real poems are very rarely produced. Most of the so-called poems are nothing but verses. So if we try to define poetry, we would be reducing the scope of poetry itself.

Poetry is an expression of imagination and when it is conveyed with some rhyme and musical quality, it will have a lasting effect. Without that musical quality or melody, poetry will not appeal. Moreover, poetry should be written in such a way that it should disturb our minds, it should unsettle whatever is there in our minds and unless poetry is a thought-provoking one, we cannot say that it is a poem. Mere description can never be a poem at all. There are some old and worn out ideas in our minds. By reading a poem, those ideas should be unsettled, they should be disturbed. If the lines do not appeal to our hearts, it is not a poem.

Why do you write poetry?

Writing poetry is purely creative, and it gives me so much pleasure and happiness. It gives me immense delight which cannot be described or expressed in words. And that is why, in order to forget the exhaustion and tiresomeness of the professional life, I spend my time in my creative writing.

Nature is always present in your poems. Are you influenced by the English Romantic poets?

Yes, I was very much influenced by the British Romantic poets. Right from the good old days, even when I was a student, I was fond of Romantic Poetry—the poetry of Wordsworth, Shelley and Keats. Naturally, it had made a deep impression on me. Moreover, I was born and brought up in a village which was surrounded on all sides by the beauty of nature. So the influence of my surroundings was there deeply on me. That is why I was very much impressed and began drawing so much of joy in describing the objects of Nature which I saw.

What do you think 'art is for art's sake' or 'art is for morality's sake'?

These two schools appear to be two different ends, but at one stage they merge together. They get united. Even though a poet writes for himself or for his own pleasure, he happens to be a member of the society. Therefore, in whatever he writes, he will be communicating something that would be good and useful to the well-being of the people at large and that will be the message to the society.

Among the English poets who do you like most?

I like the Romantic poets, especially the poems of Keats. His odes are very beautiful. Among them, Ode to a Nightingale, Ode to Autumn, Ode to a Grecian Urn - are three jewels. His poems reveal deeper feelings and emotions, and moreover, even as a young man he succeeded in articulating his feelings in unforgettable words.

You have written so many beautiful poems. Do you have any special one to mention?

There are poems such as Lake at Night, Thousand Pillars, Swamiji and Indian Bride. These are some of my very good poems.

You have written an English grammar book. Tell us a bit about the book.

Yes, the book gives the basic principles and rules of grammar aiming at the improvement of essential language skills as reading and writing in English; it was prescribed for all the UG students of the entire State of Andhra Pradesh and it was there for six years.

Professional works and creative writing - how do you manage two sides?

During the daytime my entire professional work would be over and during nights I would be totally free. I would be awake till the midnight hour and I would be just writing and writing.

You are a novelist. Tell us something about your novels?

So far, I have written only two novels. Both the novels are about the rural life, and I feel that no English novelist has completely delved deep into the subject of the presentation of rural life and that gap I wanted to fill. In my own modest way, I think I have filled the gap. The common people, small farmers and peasants are my subject. Exploitation of the poor farmers by the landlords and also the depravity and degeneration among the poor people- are main themes of my novels.

What is your message to young poets?

The young poets are showing so much talent. I feel really proud of them. They cannot be overlooked or ignored at all. The first thing they need is proper encouragement. There are so many promising poets in our country. If they are given proper encouragement and atmosphere, naturally they will shine; but they should be quality-conscious.

Do you have any message for society?

We are all children of Nature. We should never neglect Nature. At the same time, we should keep our society clean and free from corruption.

See more at: http://www.merinews.com/article/in-conversation-with-famous-indian-poet-dr-vasudeva-reddy/15882185.shtml#sthash.un2HGyMC.dpuf

About the Author

Dr .T. Vasudeva Reddy, born in Dec. 1943 in a village near the famous pilgrim town Tirupati in Andhra State in India, did M.A in English in 1966 and got Ph. D. for his thesis on the novels of Jane Austen. He worked as Lecturer, Reader and U.G.C National Fellow and Visiting Professor, and retired as Principal of Govt. Degree College in Dec. 2001 and later as Principal of prestigious Post-Graduate colleges. He received the Awards of International Eminent Poet in 1987, Hon. D. Litt. from the WAAC, San Francisco in 1988, Best Teacher Award at the College & University level from the Govt. of A.P. in 1990, Best Poetry award for his third poetry book *The Fleeting Bubbles* from Michael Madhusudan Dutt Academy, Calcutta in 1994 and the prestigious U.G.C Award of National Fellowship in 1998. His biography figures in the American Biographical Institute (N. Carolina, USA), International Biographical Institute (Cambridge), Reference India & Asia (New Delhi) and Sahitya Akademi (New Delhi).

He is a renowned poet, critic and novelist of international repute. His poems appeared in French journals in Paris. M.Phil. and Ph.D. theses have been produced on his works. He received the international Award of "Excellence in World Poetry" in 2009. He is now Hon. President of GIEWEC (Guild of Indian English Writers Editors and Critics). He is an internationally recognized poet in English with 11 poetry books to his credit. His poetic career spans over a long period of three and a half decades from 1982 till now and his creative quill knows no rest. He is at once a realistic and romantic poet, a lover of nature and a poet with social commitment, a lyricist and a satirist aiming at the improvement of ethical standards.

As Prof. David Kerr of Monash Univ. Australia says, "T.V. Reddy is a real poet with a commitment to perfection….His poetry is an outburst of emotion and it succeeds in creating the basic human feelings." In the words of Prof. Nissim Ezekiel, a distinguished Indian poet, "Like a gifted sculptor he chisels his poems with the deftness of a master craftsman."

Other Works

Poetry:

When Grief Rains (New Delhi, Samakaleen Pubs., 1982)
The Broken Rhythms (Madras, Poets Press, 1987)
The Fleeting Bubbles (Madras, Poets Press, 1989)
Melting Melodies (Madras, Poets Press, 1994)
Pensive Memories (Madras, Poets Press, 2005)
Gliding Ripples (U.S.A., Baltimore, Pub. America, 2008)
Echoes (N. Delhi, Authors Press, 2012)
Quest for Peace (N. Delhi, Authors Press, 2013)
Golden Veil (N. Delhi, Authors Press, 2016)
Thousand Haiku Pearls (N. Delhi, Authors Press, 2016)
Sound and Silence (N.Delhi, AuthorsPress, 2017)
The Rural Muse: The Poetry of T.Vasudeva Reddy. Ed. K.V. Raghupathi (N. Delhi, Authors Press, 2014).

Novels:

The Vultures (Calcutta, Golden Books, 1983)
Minor Gods (New York, 2008)

Criticism:

Jane Austen: The Dialectics of Self-Actualization in her Novels (New Delhi, Sterling Pubs., 1987)
Jane Austen: The Matrix of Matrimony (Jaipur, Bohra Pubs., 1987)
A Critical Survey of Indo-English Poetry (N. Delhi, Authors Press, 2016).

Grammar:

Advanced Grammar & Composition in English (Hyderabad, Commonwealth Pubs., 1996)

The Essential Readings Series brings the best of Indian English Poetry to the West

K. V. Dominic Essential Readings gathers for the first time the three most important works of poetry from this shining new light of contemporary Indian verse in English: *Winged Reason, Write Son, Write* and *Multicultural Symphony*. A fourth collection of 22 previously unpublished poems round out a complete look at the first 12 years of Dominic's prolific and profound verse. Each poem includes unique Study Guide questions suitable for South Asian studies curricula.

Written in free verse, each of his poems makes the reader contemplate on intellectual, philosophical, spiritual, political, and social issues of the present world. Themes range from multiculturalism, environmental issues, social mafia, caste-ism, exploitation of women and children, poverty, and corruption to purely introspective matters. From the observation of neighborhood life to international events, and everyday forgotten tragedies of India, nothing escapes the grasp of Dominic's keen sense of the fragility of life and morality in the modern world.

"K. V. Dominic is one of the most vibrant Indian English poets whose intense passion for the burning social and national ailments makes him a disciple of Ezekielean School of poetry. His poetic passion for the natural beauty keeps him besides the Romanticists."

-- Dr. A. K. Choudhary, English poet, critic and editor,
Professor of English, Assam, India

"K. V. Dominic's poems are important additions to the growing global movement to bring about positive change and equality for all individuals. The injustices he confronts in his poems are the arrows and thorns that pierce his heart every day and the gushing blood that runs through his pen to paper."

-- Rob Harle, poet and critic, Nimbin, Australia

ISBN 978-1-61599-302-4

Modern History Press

www.ingramcontent.com/pod-product-compliance
Lightning Source LLC
Chambersburg PA
CBHW071600030726
47593CB00001BA/256